D0672412

For Mothers of Difficult Daughters

For Mothers of Difficult Daughters

HOW TO ENRICH AND REPAIR THE RELATIONSHIP IN ADULTHOOD

Dr. Charney Herst

WITH Lynette Padwa

VILLARD

New York

Author's Note

The examples and anecdotes in this book are based on real people and incidents. However, all names, ages, physical attributes, and other identifying features have been changed to protect the privacy of the participants.

Library of Congress Cataloging-in-Publication Data

Herst, Charney.

For mothers of difficult daughters: how to enrich and repair the relationship in adulthood/Charney Herst, with Lynette Padwa.

p.   cm.

Includes index.

ISBN 0-679-45765-8

1. Parent and adult child.   2. Mothers and daughters.   I. Padwa, Lynette.

HQ755.86.H47   1998

306.874—dc21   97-37268

Random House website address: www.randomhouse.com

Printed in the United States of America on acid-free paper

98765432

First Edition

Book Design by Barbara M. Bachman

In Memory of my

wonderful Mother,

Sylvia Madrazo.

—C.H.

To my parents,

Libby and Ned Padwa,

with love and gratitude.

—L.P.

ACKNOWLEDGMENTS

I wish to express my gratitude to my parents, Sylvia and Angel Madrazo. They taught me the principles of sound family life, and I have endeavored to follow the model they provided me. They inculcated within me their European values of dignity and respect along with unconditional love, nurturance, and acceptance. I passed these fundamentals of family on to my children.

I am grateful to my husband, Simon, for his patience, understanding, support, and excellent spelling ability. He is my best friend and president of my fan club.

To my big brother, David Louis Madrazo, thank you for parenting me when I needed it. To my little sister, Paula Rudy, thank you for allowing me to parent you. We developed these skills at an early age. Along with my half brothers Larry and Murray Gray, and Grandma Ethel Lubinsky, we comprised a big, healthy, spirited, cooperative family.

To my children, thank you for helping me to become the person I am today. From you I learned patience and tolerance for almost everything, never letting go of our family love and all of its benefits. My best education came from you five. We are a living textbook. My family: Robin Stevens, David Herst, Rick Herst, Barbara Einseidl, and Helene Bixler. Their mates respectively: John Brammel, Andrea Paparides, Susan Herst, Richard Einseidl, and Larry Bixler. I am grateful for my stepchildren: Robert Buchsbaum and his wife, Dona, and Jeffrey Buchsbaum and his mate, Richard Ginzel. Thank you for the grandchildren you have contributed to the family: Rebecca Goodman, Douglas Yonkich, Rick Jr. and Linzy Herst; William, Daniel, and Ashley Bixler; and Jennifer Buchsbaum, our latest addition.

Thanks to Dr. Phoebe Frank, my dearest friend, for her inspiration. She served as a good example, having already been published. To Dr. Barbara Griffith, who so professionally edited the book's technical aspects, I am grateful. To Dr. Martin Bravin, my mentor and friend and colleague, thank you for always believing in me. To my readers, Shellie and Len Liebson and Helen and Al Dennis, thank you for valuable feedback. To Joan Kossowsky, my very first friend from my hometown, Perth Amboy, N.J., I am grateful for our lifelong friendship. Our mothers were friends and they brought us together when we were five. To my girlfriends Lil Bleifer and Paquita Pierpont, I am still delighted with your mother stories.

To the ladies who read: Thank you for your valuable mother-daughter stories. Every thought you shared helped my process in this book. Monday book club members: Millie Polisky, Charlotte Rothman, Mickey Keyser, Myrna Eiduson, Bertie Massoth, Chickie Abel, and Marion Cohen. Thursday book club members: Phoebe Frank, Audrey Buchsbaum, Harriet Oppenheim, Barbara Swedelson, Bobbie Klubeck, Lois Treiser, and Allegreta Blau.

To my adopted family, I am grateful to all of you for your support and enthusiasm: Allen and Marcia Turner, Lee Lupoff, Rita Borne, Barbara and Al Swedelson, Harriet amd Irwin Oppenheim, Lori and Arthur Stelzer, Rabbi Jerry, and Mickey Fisher.

I wish to express my heartfelt appreciation to Leslie Berger of the *Los Angeles Times.* Leslie wrote an article about the clinical work I do in my practice with groups and private clients having mother-daughter problems. Suzanne Wickham-Beaird of Random House, editor of this book, was one of the many people who read that article. Suzanne has since become my patron, adviser, my support system, and my guide into the literary world. An exemplary person, Suzanne in her warm, comforting way managed to shelter me while at the same time professionally and skillfully moving me through the maze of publication. I am proud to know her.

Betsy Amster, agent supreme, handles the myriad details of the huge undertaking called "the book." This is a complicated process to learn and Betsy was always there to act as guide and cheerleader. Thank you, Betsy.

My writer, collaborator, colleague, friend, and surrogate daughter, Lynette Padwa, is very important to me. Not only did we become a writing team, we also became very close in our relationship. It is so comforting to know that your working partner is someone you love, trust, and respect. She is an excellent writer, and I would have been lost and overwhelmed without her. I hope she will always be in my life.

Finally I want to express my appreciation to the 150 or more mothers and daughters I have spoken to about their relationships. They are the heroines, since it is their lives and stories that make up the substance of this volume. Thank you all for your cooperation and openness. You will not recognize yourselves since all identifying features have been changed; just remember that each of you has contributed greatly to this book.

—DR. CHARNEY HERST

CONTENTS

Introduction

We stood in the courtroom, my teenage daughter and I, staring up at the judge seated on his bench high above us. The year was 1970 and my daughter was the reason we were there—unbeknownst to me, she had planted marijuana in my rose garden. A neighbor child had stolen a plant and taken it home, where his mother promptly discovered it and reported us to the police. Our whole family was charged with possession of an illegal drug. After hearing my testimony, the judge peered over at me reproachfully and ordered, "Mother, get your act together."

"Me?" I blurted out. "*She* planted it!" Stung and humiliated, I was furious at the judge for his unfair assumptions. But I should have thanked him, for in that moment a mother's advocate was born.

At the time the judge issued his sage advice, I was the mother of five teenagers. I was a Boy Scout troop mother, carpool driver, housekeeper for a ten-room house, breeder of collies, and I held a straight-A average in the college courses I was taking during the day when my kids were in school. My "act" was together. It was my daughter's actions that were the problem. Yet I was admonished and publicly embarrassed, especially after the local newspaper ran the story—complete with a photo of my rose garden.

In retrospect it's humorous, but back then I felt utterly shamed. Our lawyer was able to get the charges dropped because our privacy had been invaded, but the incident stayed with me. I vowed that when I had completed my education and my youngsters were out on their own, I'd try in my own small way to stage a mother's revolt. Despite what the judge and most of the psychiatric community preached, I knew one simple truth: It's not all

Mom's fault. We mothers share responsibility for our children's upbringing with our husbands, extended families, and with the society and era in which they grow up. Perhaps most important, our children are individuals. We cannot control their actions or create their personalities. All we can do is try our best to raise them and love them well.

When my children were grown, I did complete my education, eventually earning a Ph.D. in Psychology. I've been in practice for twenty-five years now, and one of my main focuses has been mothers and their adult daughters. Far too many of the rebellious girls from the 1960s and '70s—my weed-growing daughter's comrades in spirit—grew up to be angry, unhappy women, and too many of their mothers still wrestle with guilt. Fifteen or twenty years later, they are still wondering where they failed their daughters, what they did wrong. It's no surprise they blame themselves: for the past thirty years, most psychologists have held Mom responsible for her child's personality. Our daughters, often at the urging of their therapists, reason that their unhappiness has been caused by a bad childhood—which basically translates to bad mothering. No one has been there to speak up for Mom, and I am determined to do so. I am on a mission to regain for Mother some of the respect she deserves.

In private sessions and mothers' support groups, I have tried to instill in these mothers, who are now in their fifties, sixties, and seventies, a sense of self-confidence and perspective. I've worked with daughters, mothers, and both together; I've given seminars and workshops; I speak wherever they'll have me in order to spread my message: Mothers and daughters are individuals. The bond between them is sacred and indestructible, but they are still individuals, each responsible for their own actions and fate. By acknowledging this individuality, accepting responsibility for themselves, and respecting each other as adults and equals, mothers and daughters can work through their old resentments and build a new kind of relationship together.

In 1996, the *Los Angeles Times* ran a story about one of my support groups, Mothers of Difficult Daughters. Suzanne Wickham-Beaird, West Coast editor of Villard Books, saw the story and approached me about doing this book. It's based on my experiences counseling moms and daughters, interviews with many women, my reading of every book in print on the subject of mothers and daughters, and countless hours spent comparing notes with other professionals.

The book categorizes difficult daughters according to types—dependent, dissatisfied, and distant—but in real life, personality traits are not so distinct. Types overlap and problems are multilayered, which is why it's essential to read the whole book from beginning to end, no matter what main category your daughter falls into. Otherwise you'll miss important concepts and lose the philosophical thread of the book. Read it all the way through, then reread. Make notes and underline key passages.

We've tried to write a book that's down-to-earth and free of psychological jargon, because we want you to absorb the message. There are tales of humor and woe in these pages, and there's a lot of hard work to be done. As mothers and daughters both know, there is no bond more intimate than the one they share. It's same-sex, it lasts a lifetime, and it can be intensely rewarding or brutally painful. When a relationship this profound goes awry, it takes effort to get it back on track. But time, compassion, and the solutions offered here can take you and your daughter to new levels of understanding and friendship. I've seen it happen scores of times in my own practice, and it can happen for you, too. Never give up hope!

—DR. CHARNEY HERST

PART ONE

MOTHERS AND DAUGHTERS,

IN IT FOR THE LONG RUN

CHAPTER ONE

What Did I Do Wrong?

I remember driving my daughter to ballet class and baking tray upon tray of chocolate-chip cookies for her Brownie troop. I chauffeured her to piano lessons, tap dance, swimming, art class, modeling school . . . am I leaving anything out? Oh yes: I didn't allow her to camp out at the beach when she was in ninth grade. She still brings it up, as if this were some form of child abuse.

—Liddy, age fifty-four

EVERY WOMAN HAS A MOTHER STORY. IF YOU BEGIN A sentence with the words, "My mother—," nine times out of ten the person you're talking to will jump in before you're finished, anxious to tell you about *her* mother. Mom was too pushy, or too weak. She was demanding, or neglectful. Mom loved me too much, or too little. That's why I'm so messed up.

Bookstores are stuffed with tomes offering advice to damaged daughters; therapists' couches sag with the weight of grumpy "adult children." In the therapy-happy 1970s and '80s, women were encouraged to view their mothers as nearly godlike, wielding awesome power over their daughter's self-esteem and happiness. In the 1990s, mothers are still being blamed for everything that's gone wrong in their grown daughters' lives. But where is the other side of the story? Where are the mothers' voices?

Their stories are in my office—and in this book.

For twenty-five years I've been counseling mothers and their grown daughters, trying to bring together women who see each other as rivals, martyrs, or manipulators, but rarely as equals. I've listened to hundreds of daughters complain (often rightfully) about their mothers' unreasonable or unkind behavior. But at the same time I've gotten a firsthand look at the current generation of daughters, and the picture is not encouraging.

Our daughters' expectations are grand: Shouldn't Mom always be there for me, no matter how old I am? Shouldn't she accept me unconditionally? Shouldn't she put my needs before hers?

Our daughters' assumptions are naïve: Moms naturally know how to raise children. Moms don't have problems. Moms love to take care of other people.

Our daughters' memories are long: Why did you make me wear orthopedic shoes in the fifth grade? Why did you take my hamster back to the pet store? Why did you throw out my favorite pair of overalls?

Mothers, for the most part, are angry and baffled. "Why can't my daughter grow up and get over it?" they ask me. And yes, many daughters do seem to cling to their victim status, even if it means sacrificing a closeness that both mother and daughter genuinely desire.

Family Secrets

When I first decided to become a therapist in 1973, I was already sensitive to the subject of mothers and daughters. At the time I was struggling with five teenagers, each enthralled by the counterculture of the 1960s. My three daughters provided "challenges" ranging from the mundane to the spectacular, so before I ever entered the university I had already looked to the experts for advice. I was painfully aware of their views on childhood development: any problems a child might have—autism, homosexuality, schizophrenia, lags in development, learning disabilities, acting out—were the mother's fault. According to the professionals, my mothering was at the root of my daughters' angry rebelliousness. The influence of the sixties, the widespread use of drugs, the confusing sexual mores, and even the fact that their father had died when the girls were young, all paled in comparison, supposedly, to my influence on them.

In those days, having problems with your children was shameful. You kept it a secret, especially if you were an aspiring psychologist. Who would go to a therapist who couldn't raise healthy kids? So I stayed quiet and did my own research, trying to cobble together a way to deal with the furor that raged in our household. For some reason, I knew instinctively that I wasn't solely to blame, no matter what the psychology books said. I hadn't been a perfect parent, but I loved my children with all my heart and told them so. There was always food on the table, warmth in the house, loving support, and an opportunity to talk. I knew in my soul that I'd been a good mom, and whatever mistakes I might have made, they didn't add up to the problems I was now having with the girls.

One day when I was in graduate school I decided to get brave. I had been in group therapy for about a year, a required part of the graduate program in clinical psychology. In that year I had never once mentioned that I was struggling with my daughters; I was far too embarrassed. Now I trusted the group enough to reveal my secret and perhaps get some empathy or suggestions from them.

"I've been having a lot of trouble with my girls," I confessed, and mentioned a recent episode where one of my daughters had been caught with drugs.

In an instant, the group turned on me. "You must have neglected your daughters," one women declared.

"I love my daughters," I protested. "I've done everything I could for them."

"You must have caused this problem somehow," another student chimed in. "What did you do wrong? Did you really want children?"

And so it went that day, as one group member after another offered an opinion about my inadequacy, my "hidden rage," my errors. Sure, they diagnosed my situation from a psychoanalytic stance using all the latest terminology, but I was brutalized just the same. I felt abandoned and attacked. The group leader, who was the only one who had known about my problems, stood silently by and let them jump me.

Later I confronted him: "Why didn't you defend me?" He admitted I was right—he should have intervened. That he didn't is just one small example of the pressure everyone felt to toe the psychology line and blame Mother for her child's behavior.

Help for Moms Like Me

The daughter with whom I had the most trouble back then is now an adult. She's my most caring and dutiful child; I hear from her more often than any of my other children, and she plans every family celebration. Time and love, plus a lot of effort on both sides, changed my angry, uncontrollable girl into a well-adjusted woman and delightful companion.

In the first few years of my practice, I acted on faith that this would eventually occur. As I worked on my relationships with my own daughters, I carefully charted the case histories of the mothers and daughters who were my clients. Although my practice was not—and still is not—limited to mothers and daughters, theirs were the most compelling stories, the ones I really took to heart. I wanted to help both mothers and daughters, but over time I became more focused on the mothers' points of view. For one thing, mothers had nobody in their corner. The literature and research all came from the daughters' perspective. Someone had to take the mothers' side, and since I had lived through it myself, I was eager to be that person. These moms needed a visible, vocal advocate, and I've become that.

As the years passed and my practice grew, I began to notice that the troubled mother-daughter relationships seemed to fall across a continuum. At one end were the *dependent daughters,* whose lives and identities were so enmeshed with their mothers' that both women felt smothered and furious at the other. At the opposite end were the *distant daughters,* who rejected everything about their mothers, often refusing to visit or even telephone them. In between were less extreme cases, mothers and daughters who were still talking to each other but who both felt unhappy with the relationship. I call the daughters in this group *dissatisfied daughters.* Nothing ever seems to go right for them; they're always irritable, unhappy, and disagreeable, and their mothers spend hours each day listening to their complaints and trying to solve their problems.

In this book, I'm going to share with you the techniques I've developed for mothers of difficult daughters. With these methods, you'll be able to reshape your relationship with your grown daughter, starting today. I'll help you discover the reasons why things have gone wrong between the two of you, beginning with an honest look at your expectations and hers. I'll reveal the insights I've gleaned from hundreds of hours counseling moms and daughters. Through exercises and case histories, you may finally understand why your daughter can't seem to let go of you, or why you can't fix her unhappiness, or why she still feels betrayed by events that occurred decades ago. But understanding is only half the solution—you'll also get the tools to reconnect with your daughter and try to build a new, more realistic, more loving relationship with her.

No matter what type of daughter you have—dependent, dissatisfied, or distant—or how tense your relationship has become, there is an excellent chance you can turn things around. My methods have worked for hundreds of women, and they can work for you, too. As I tell the distraught mothers who seek my help each week, "Never, never stop trying. Where's there's love, there's hope."

The Myths of Motherhood

The mothers and daughters I counsel come in every shape, age, and color. Within the dependent, dissatisfied, and distant groups there are, of course, dozens of variations. So I was more than a little surprised to realize, after studying them for several years, that these diverse pairs all had one thing in common: The daughters and mothers all had bought into the myth of the perfect mom.

Most mothers and daughters unconsciously assume that somewhere, in some far-off, white clapboard house, there lives a perfect family. In that family, Mom behaves the way a good mother should. Her ideal code of behavior is seldom spelled out, but here are some of her supposed attributes, gathered from the women I've counseled.

Mothers are always available.
Mothers are forever generous.
Mothers are always supportive.
Mothers are unconditionally accepting.
Mothers do not have problems of their own.
Mothers do not get angry.
Mothers do not complain.
Mothers are an endless source of nurturance.
Mothers naturally know how to raise children.
Mothers always put their child's needs first, no matter how old the child.
Mothers are always strong.

It sounds like a tough job description when it's set down in black and white. But not only do daughters believe their mothers should meet these standards; most of the mothers agree! Show them this list, and they'd deny it. But when a mom confides to me a specific problem with her daughter, she'll reflexively revert to self-blame: she wasn't supportive enough, calm enough, insightful enough. In the end, most mothers are still trying to be the faultless, flawless, perfect mom. They are unable to accept themselves as is.

"Saint Mom" Is a Recent Invention

Mothers weren't always held to such unrealistic standards. For most of human history, childrearing was far less romantic. Women of the upper classes usually foisted their children off on wet nurses and nannies, then shipped them to boarding schools when they reached puberty (if not sooner). An article in *The Journal of the American Medical Association* in 1896 bemoaned the fact that upper-class ladies didn't want to become mothers at all—motherhood got in the way of their partying. Divorce rates were soaring, claimed the article, because husbands found themselves "bound to women to whom sexual relations are repugnant, whose horror of maternity is overpowering."

Working-class women, meanwhile, struggled with the arduous job of running a household, which in those days required the energy of an army commander. These moms had little time for "coddling" a child. One mother, who lived in Minnesota in the 1870s, described in her diary a typical day. She woke early and "baked six loaves of bread. Made a kettle of mush and have now a suet pudding and beef boiling . . . I have managed to put my clothes away and set my house in order. . . . Nine o'clock P.M. was delivered of another son." Back then, mothers bore many children, each of whom was expected to pull his or her weight.

I'm not suggesting that children were better off being sent to boarding school or vying with seven siblings for their mother's attention. On the surface, intense devotion from Mom would seem to be a better way, one that ought to produce confident, happy children. But the stream of disgruntled, resentful daughters who accompany their mothers into my office implies otherwise. Were "adult children" this troubled a century ago? I have no way of knowing, nor can I guess how content these grown sons and daughters were compared to today's adults. I do know that in the 1800s neither upper- nor working-class mothers spent their lives hovering over their children, yet mothers were respected far more at that time than they are today.

Whatever Happened to "Honor Thy Mother"?

As little as fifty years ago, mothers were admired as hard-working, indispensable heads of the household. Even if you weren't especially fond of your mother, you honored her, as the Old Testament decreed. That sort of respect has all but vanished. As we've demanded more of Mother, and as psychologists have insisted that she alone can make or break us, our regard for her has plummeted. Why?

One reason might be that we would resent anyone who held that much control over us. We'd try to knock her down, to undercut her power. The best way to do this is to make fun of her. Books, films, TV programs, popular songs, and advertising are filled with unflattering images of Mom the meddler, Mom the manipulator, Mom the eagle-eyed critic. The thread running through all of it is Mom's power—even the most wizened Jewish mother has the ability to undo her lawyer-daughter or CEO-son by commenting on her weight or his girlfriend. Mom wields her power mercilessly, but at the same time she's a petty character, someone who has nothing better to do with her time than nose in on her children's business.

The guffaws at Mom's expense are not limited to the media. I see it in everyday life, too: daughters are prone to giving their moms cutesy nicknames such as "Chubs," designed to take her down a notch or two. They poke fun at her hairstyle ("Maybe you'll change it sometime this decade"), her clothes ("Ma! Didn't you wear that to my ninth-grade recital?"), her friends, her food, her memory loss. Their feelings for their mothers are a mixture of loving tolerance and disappointment that she didn't live up to their idealized standard of the perfect mom. Add to that their suspicion that Mom has somehow hobbled their potential, and these grown daughters have a lot of resentment brewing. Everyone, moms included, should be able to take a little good-natured ribbing. But there is a relentlessness to these gibes that disturbs me. Laughter is not always the best medicine—it can be cruel, even toxic.

In addition to being a backlash against Mom's alleged power, the disrespect for Mom has much to do with our swiftly changing culture. Researchers in the U.S. and Great Britain have noticed that in families with strong ethnic or religious ties Mother is still respected. I've seen this in my own practice: Among families who have recently arrived in Los Angeles from Mexico, Central America, or Asia, mothers are regarded with affection and admiration, and Mother's name is proudly defended. In a related set of studies, researchers in London focused on the mother-daughter bond among working-class women. They found that these bonds were strong until the families became more affluent, at which point the respect for family, and Mother, dwindled.

It seems that as people grow more assimilated or upwardly mobile, their attention turns to their friends, spouse, and children, and away from their parents and extended family. Maybe second-generation immigrants are ashamed of their parents and want to distance themselves from their folks' quaint, unfashionable ways. Perhaps it's because we live in a terribly transient society, where grandparents, aunts, and uncles are infrequent guests in our homes, little more than agreeable strangers. Maybe it's because some Americans place so much emphasis on youth and money and so little on family and tradition. Whatever the reasons—and it's beyond the scope of this book to explain them—it seems clear that Mom and Dad are going to have to establish a new place for themselves within this changing social structure. Will moms be companions, friends, consultants, consciences? You, as a mother, will have to define your own role.

Our culture's shifting expectations coupled with the mom-blaming school of psychotherapy have put mothers in a double bind. Young mothers are censured for going to work instead of devoting 100 percent of their time to raising their children, while older moms who *did* devote 100 percent of their time to raising their kids are held accountable for their children's shortcomings. As mothers try to improve their relationships with their grown daughters, they often waver between impatience with their daughters' accusations and a lingering, guilty feeling that they must have somehow failed them. It seems the eighteen years they spent raising their daughters earned them neither their gratitude nor their respect. What happened?

Letting Moms off the Hook

The mothers I counsel always ask me the same question when we sit down for our first session. "What did I do wrong?" they plead. "Help me so I can fix it."

"If you didn't batter, abuse, or neglect your daughter—if you loved her and provided warmth and support—you did nothing wrong," I respond. Many moms have a hard time accepting this revolutionary idea.

"But I must have done *something*," they insist.

"Not necessarily," I say—and I have the scientific data to prove it.

Nearly every mental condition that was once ascribed to bad mothering has turned out to be either genetic or caused by the biochemical makeup of the brain. Homosexuality is the most famous example: Freud declared that male homosexuality was caused by a domineering mother and an absent father, and this diagnosis was accepted for most of this century. In 1973, the

American Psychiatric Association (APA) decided that homosexuality was not a mental illness after all, and removed it from the *Diagnostic and Statistical Manual of Mental Disorders,* second edition, the field's Bible. More important than the APA's opinion, however, are recent findings that strongly suggest that a region of the X chromosome may determine male homosexuality. In addition, studies have shown that an area of the brain, the anterior hypothalamus, is more than twice as large in heterosexual men as in homosexual men. Whether Mom is Blanche DuBois or Bella Abzug doesn't matter a whit.

Another harrowing example of misplaced mother blame concerns autism. Bruno Bettelheim, a highly esteemed psychoanalyst, specialized in treating autistic children and announced in his 1967 book, *The Empty Fortress,* that "the precipitating factor in infantile autism is the parent's wish that his child should not exist." As it turns out, "conscious or unconscious [parental] attitudes . . . experienced by the child as the wish that he did not exist" have zero to do with the illness. Instead, current research suggests that a complex set of conditions within the brain causes a wide array of symptoms we call autism. The causes of the disease remain largely a mystery, but Bettelheim's theory has quietly disappeared. Today few would dream of suggesting that a child is autistic because his parents didn't properly bond with him.

Nature versus Nurture News

These and countless other mental disorders once blamed on Mom are now known to have biochemical or genetic roots. That doesn't mean, however, that environment and family have no effect on a child's mental health. Mothers and fathers do have an impact, but the question is, how much? That's the ancient dilemma about nature versus nurture, and it's not likely to be solved in our lifetime. Still, it remains one of the most fascinating questions in psychology, and many researchers devote their careers to teasing out clues from the most reliable source: twins.

Twins who have been separated at birth and raised in different environments offer us our only real opportunity to gauge how much a person's upbringing affects his or her personality. In the May 1997 edition of *The APA Monitor*, the American Psychological Association announced: "Nature, nurture: not mutually exclusive." The front-page article reported that studies on twins and adopted children conducted over the past twenty years have "firmly established that there is a genetic component to just about every human trait and behavior, including personality, general intelligence and behavioral disorders such as schizophrenia and autism. . . . Genetics account, on average, for half of the variance of most traits." The environment, including not just Mother but everything and every person a child experiences, accounts for the other half.

"This does not mean that there are no purely environmental effects on behavior," the article points out. For example, researchers found that the loss of a parent during childhood is directly correlated with depression in women. Indeed, everyone in the field of psychology agrees that a traumatic childhood can permanently damage a child. Traumas such as war, severe poverty, neglect, and mental, physical, or sexual abuse can warp a developing personality. The damage may take the form of depression, dissociation, or a host of other mental illnesses—often the same illnesses that in other people are caused by biochemical imbalances or genetic traits.

Trauma alters personality, but how many among us have been deeply traumatized? When I was studying psychology, we were schooled on the famous British studies conducted by René Spitz, John Bowlby, and D. W. Winnicott. These researchers studied babies in orphanages who were severely neglected by their caretakers and were cut off from all human contact. The infants lay in individual cribs, with sheets covering the cribs so that they were deprived even of the sight of other babies. These poor children eventually refused to eat and often died from neglect. H. F. Harlow's work with monkeys deprived of maternal contact underscored these studies.

But my fellow graduate students and I were not treating clients who had spent their infancy in isolated, sheet-covered cribs. Except for a few cases of abuse, the clients we saw came from average homes, with parents who had loved them and neither neglected nor abused them. Yet we—and the great majority of psychologists practicing today—were taught to apply the findings of these neglected-baby studies to the adult clients we treated. We were told to start off counseling sessions with queries such as "What was it like growing up in your home?" or "Tell me about your mother."

To most people, these seem like perfectly natural questions. *Of course* if your daughter has a problem—say, with decision making—it must be because you somehow gave her the wrong signals or failed to be a positive role model. But as familiar as this reasoning feels, it's just as likely that she was born with an indecisive nature. Unless you battered her or told her each day that she was worthless, your treatment of her is less relevant than how she is genetically predisposed to react to that treatment. Remember, you were only a part of her environment, and environment only accounts for half of her personality traits. In most cases, Mom is not to blame for a daughter who can't sustain friendships, or succeed in a career, or lose weight.

So What Is My Daughter's Problem— and Can I Fix It?

By the time a mother works up the courage to seek my help, she is usually pretty certain that there is something atypical about her daughter's behavior. Otherwise, she reasons, the two of them would have been able to call a truce by this time. After all, these are mothers of grown daughters, not teenagers. The mothers I counsel range in age from their mid-forties all the way up to their eighties. Some of the daughters are in their fifties. These troubles have been simmering for years, sometimes decades.

I urge these moms to at least consider the possibility that they aren't entirely responsible for their daughters' states of mind. That's the first step in relieving some of their anguish, but it still leaves a big question: If I'm not the problem, what is?

There's no easy answer, of course. Every situation is different. Throughout this book I'll do my best to explain the difficult-daughter phenomenon and offer my advice about the most common problems, yet one truth remains constant for every situation: *You do not have to fix your daughter's problems to improve your relationship with her.* In fact, you can't fix her problems. Only she can do that. You have to fix yourself, and at the same time learn how to respond to her problems with clarity and forethought.

Your daughter's mental health is a separate issue from your relationship with her, no matter how entwined the two might become. I can think of no better example of this than the story of Alda, whose daughter had cerebral palsy and was emotionally disturbed. Fortunately, most of us do not have to deal with so serious a problem; that's why the advice in this book is geared toward mothers whose daughters are functioning in the outside world. But Alda's case shows how, even in extreme circumstances, a mother can improve her relationship with her daughter by changing her own perspective.

Alda's daughter, Louise, had been in and out of nursing homes for most of her life. Alda was in a perpetual state of mourning over the loss of her daughter and her own helplessness in the situation. Louise called Alda several times each day to complain about the horrible treatment she was receiving at the hands of the staff. She was medicated, so she was pain-free and the other severe symptoms of her condition were under control. However, Louise was a rebellious woman who got evicted from one facility after another. Her dress was bizarre and her demeanor ribald; she chain-smoked and dumped her food tray daily. No one wanted her around, even though her palsy was getting worse. No one felt sorry for her except Alda.

By the time she was in her early thirties, Louise had been in and out of more than twenty board-and-care institutions. After explaining Louise's background to me, Alda broke down and sobbed, confiding that her daily talks with her daughter were breaking her heart.

"She's like a lost soul," wept Alda.

"No she's not," I argued. "*You* are the lost soul. Look at how powerful your daughter is. Every institution she's been in, she's managed to control the people who are supposed to be controlling her. Every place she goes she tells them what medication is fit for her—she knows better than they do. She's bright and articulate and has a terrific sense of humor. She's not physically or emotionally able to live in the outside world, but within her structured world she's master of her destiny."

Alda had never considered this possibility; she had never seen her daughter's strength. As for the daily calls, I advised Alda to set a time limit on them. "Lots of daughters call their moms once a day to let off steam," I said. "Treat it as an inevitable, but not dreadful, part of your day. Make it a controlled, timed conversation at your convenience."

Reframe it. Look at it from a different direction. "Walk through the door backwards," I tell mothers. It worked for Alda, who has finally stopped crying over her daughter. The strength she was able to see in Louise freed her to have a less pitying, more normal relationship with her. Now she jokes about how Louise planned a patient revolt, and admits she's impressed with her daughter's talent for manipulating her "handlers." "My clever daughter is at it again," she says.

Relationships Work Both Ways

I am undeniably in the mother's corner when it comes to problems between mothers and daughters. After all, daughters have a whole society—not to mention most therapists—supporting their claims that they were damaged by Mom. At the same time, I realize that there are two sides to every story. A mother must accept this if she truly wants to change her relationship with her daughter. She must learn to listen and stop defending herself when her daughter speaks. She has to agree to face some painful truths in order to resolve their problems. Her daughter has to do the same.

There are no good guys and bad guys on this road. As I often say to my clients, "Put your hurt feelings in your wastebasket and toss them out. The only thing that matters now is making up." If you can't admit when you've been too harsh or critical, if you're not willing to forgive and to ask your daughter for her forgiveness, you are not ready to take this step. Maybe you don't miss her enough. If so, read this book again in six months, and you may see things differently.

Abusive Mothers

If I could, I would hang a big red banner over every shelf where this book is displayed for sale. It would read: ABUSIVE, BATTERING, NEGLECTFUL MOTHERS—THIS BOOK IS NOT FOR YOU! In my private and group counseling sessions, there is no need for such a banner. Abusive mothers rarely return after the first visit. They realize instantly that they will not receive absolution from me for their sins against their daughters. Joint therapy can help some of these mothers and daughters, but theirs are not the cases I specialize in. The solutions in this book do not apply to families where the mother physically battered, neglected, or psychologically abused her children.

I'm aware that the term *abuse,* especially when it comes to psychological abuse, is somewhat subjective. I can't determine for every reader whether or not her family falls into the abusive category, but I can assure you that the techniques I offer in these pages will not resolve problems stemming from real abuse.

The Goals of This Book

In my work with mothers, I always have two goals: to show them how to rebuild the bond with their daughters and to help them grow as individuals. Before I can do either, I ask my clients to take an honest look at their expectations of themselves as mothers. To do that, they need to recall their relationship with their own mother, to remember the lessons, good and bad, that they learned from her about mothering. In chapter two we'll explore your mother's legacy so you can get a better understanding of the way you judge yourself as a mom.

You'll also need to clarify your expectations of your daughter—what it is about her that makes you feel proud, disappointed, anxious, angry. Equally important, you must try to discover what your daughter expects of you. Unrealistic expectations on both sides have a lot to do with the bitterness I see so often between mothers and daughters. In chapter three I'll lead you through this process of discovery.

After these forays into expectations and motivations, we'll delve into the meat of the book: solving your problems with your dependent, dissatisfied, or distant daughter. In Part V, "Moving On, Together or Alone," I'll offer suggestions for maintaining your new relationship, enhancing your life within your community, and taking charge of your future. In the Epilogue I'll hand the microphone to our daughters, letting them describe some of the challenges they've met and overcome with their moms.

Before we go any further, though, I'd like to show you the Mother's Bill of Rights. It sets out what I believe are the inalienable rights of mothers everywhere, regardless of what they or their daughters expect. Refer to it whenever you are weakening in your resolve to improve your relationship. Post it on your refrigerator or keep it on your bedside table. Most of all, commit to it. These rights are the very least you deserve.

A Mother's Bill of Rights

- I have the right to be treated with respect.
- I have the right to control my own life for as long as I can.
- I have the right to an explanation of my children's feelings—I can't intuit their thoughts.
- I have the right to be sad or angry without hiding my feelings to protect my children.
- I have the right to say no.
- I have the right to reminisce and be sentimental.
- I have the right to talk to my children about my problems. I do not expect them to provide solutions, just to listen.
- I have the right to buy nice things and go places.
- I have the right to my own opinions. I do not expect my children to agree with all of them.
- I have the right to miss my children. It does not mean I want to control them.

I have the responsibility to respect each of my children and to grant them the same rights I expect for myself.

CHAPTER TWO

Your Mother's Legacy

My mother never let me forget what she went through, giving up a career just to raise us. She was a very bright woman and I can see now why she was angry at playing errand girl to my father all her life. But she took it out on us kids, and I swore I'd never do that to my children.

— Dorothy, age fifty

By NOW, BEING A MOTHER MIGHT BE SO SECOND NATURE to you that you don't stop to wonder where your attitudes about mothering came from. But if you want to take the lead in changing your relationship with your daughter, you have to start with yourself, and that means reflecting on what you learned from your mother.

For better and for worse, your bond with your mother has directly affected your relationship with your daughter. Even if—*especially* if—your relationship with your mother has been less than glorious, you need to be aware of how it has influenced the kind of behavior you demonstrate with your daughter. As an added bonus, you might discover some valuable lessons your mother can teach you today—about loyalty, self-respect, and most of all, about how she has changed.

Your mother's legacy isn't a clear-cut list of values and instructions. It's more like a jigsaw puzzle made up of all the small experiences, along with the big lessons, you got from your mom as you were growing up. In this chapter I'm going to share with you some of the pieces of this puzzle that seem to be common to most women, in the hopes that it will help you gain insight into the problems you're having with your daughter.

Memories of Mother

Mae West once wrote of her mother, "She tried in every way to understand me, and she succeeded. It was this deep, loving understanding as long as she lived that more than anything else helped and sustained me on my way to success." West was lucky and knew it; not all women are so aware of the gifts their mothers give them. More often, we simply absorb the positive things our mothers teach us and unconsciously integrate them into our personality.

I sometimes ask my clients to tell me their fondest memories of their mothers so that they can relive some of these long-forgotten positives. One lady recalled a simple hair-washing routine: "On summer days—before air-conditioning—my mother would have me lie down on the kitchen counter with my hair falling into the sink. The countertop was cool, and the lukewarm water felt wonderful over my scalp. She took a long time lathering up my hair and rinsing it out. It felt lovely to be pampered by her."

Many women recall how they loved being cared for by Mom when they were ill. Others remember special foods their mothers prepared, songs they sang, bedtime rituals, pet names. Most of these women replayed the same foods, names, songs, and rituals with their own daughters. These, along with the thousands of details our mothers taught us about growing up female, have helped shape us as women and mothers. We pass this wealth of knowledge on to our daughters instinctively, seldom reflecting on its source.

But while our mothers' good points might fade from our consciousness, their mistakes loom large. As soon as our infant daughters are delivered in the hospital, we utter the ancient vow of mothers everywhere: "I won't make the same mistakes my mother did." And you probably won't. As the saying goes, you'll make new ones. Less obvious is the fact that your mistakes are often a result of trying to avoid hers. The ultimate irony is that, well-meaning though your efforts might be, there is a good chance your daughter won't appreciate or even notice them.

The Appreciation Gap

The huge cultural shift that's taken place in this century has caused an appreciation gap between older mothers and their adult daughters. Because motherhood is vastly different now than it was when we were growing up, many of the mistakes we sought to avoid are beyond the comprehension of our daughters.

Women who ran a household in the early part of this century did the kind of physical drudge work that today's young mothers can barely imagine. My own background is a good example. Compared to the appliance-packed homes common today, I might as well have grown up in a sod house on the prairie. We lived in a blue-collar, melting-pot neighborhood in Perth Amboy, New Jersey, and I was the middle child in a family of three children, plus Grandma in residence. After working all day in a garment factory, my mother would come home to domestic purgatory: washing clothes in a machine with a hand wringer; hanging the heavy, wet clothes and sheets to dry on a pulley clothesline tightly stretched out of a second-story window; cooking and cleaning for six people; staying up past midnight ironing. As hard as she tried, she couldn't keep up—we sometimes went without clean clothes, and we often went without lunch (mayonnaise sandwiches were standard fare at our table). My mother hated her life and complained bitterly about it to us kids. There was little joy in our house.

Sure enough, when my first daughter was born, I had my list of "nevers" all ready. "My daughter will never go hungry or want for clean clothes. I will never lay guilt trips on my daughter." And I lived up to my vows.

I hear many versions of this story in my group sessions. We women who grew up in the 1920s–1940s often were horrified at the level of self-sacrifice required of our mothers and frightened by their anger and depression. Above all, we felt guilty for causing their suffering. As a result, some of us swore never to complain to our children or blame them for our lot in life.

But do they thank us? No, they do not. How could they, when this "gift" is invisible to them? They can't know how our mothers complained to us, or imagine the kind of life we lived. They don't know what we *don't* do. If there was always food in the refrigerator when my daughters were growing up, that seemed only reasonable. If they had clean clothes, well, why shouldn't they? And it never would have occurred to my girls to be grateful that I didn't blame them for my life.

Some of the women I counsel seem to be waiting for a round of applause from their daughters for all their efforts to do things differently. I tell them, "Appreciation rarely happens the way you want it to. The words never sound quite right; they never seem like enough." My own daughters were fascinated when I revealed that, growing up, we didn't have hot water in our flat. But although it made for a good story, the difference between my life and theirs didn't really sink in. This part of my mother's legacy— my successful effort to provide for my children better than she did—is an invisible victory. The fact that my daughters lived comfortably is proof of my triumph, but I can't expect them to fully appreciate it.

In addition to the fact that your daughter has no way of comparing her life to yours, there's another reason she might not be terribly grateful to you. Ask yourself if she is actually better off for your having avoided your mother's mistakes—or were your efforts somewhat wasted? Maybe you had an absentee mother and longed for a mom who'd lavish hugs and kisses on you, only to end up with a daughter who's uncomfortable with all that close contact. Our daughters are not little clones of us, so we can't gauge their desires by what we would have wanted in a mother.

I Am You and You Are Me . . . or Are You?

The way your daughter reacts to you has a lot to do with her temperament—her God-given personality and inclinations. The same was true for you and your mother. One client of mine, Madeline, offered a poignant example of this. Her mother, a natural beauty and somewhat of a social snob, made Madeline's life miserable when she was a young girl:

> She was constantly at me to "improve myself" even
> though I was just a little kid. She wanted me to take
> horseback riding lessons, ballet lessons, to learn the flute. I
> didn't want to do any of it because, for one thing, I was a
> klutz. I had no aptitude for ballet and didn't want to ride a
> horse. I had no ear for music, either. The things I was good
> at—reading, learning, solving puzzles—had no value to my
> mother. We were a mismatch, but she told me it was my
> problem, that I was "different," meaning bad.

When Madeline had a daughter of her own, she swore to herself that she would not push an agenda on the girl. Of course, she *would* give her plenty of exposure to the things her own mother had brushed aside, such as books and educational games. But by the time little Holly was eight years old, it was clear that her interests lay elsewhere. She wanted to take tap lessons; she longed for a pony; she thrived in a group. While Holly was a wizard at making friends and socializing, she was only a mediocre student, much to Madeline's chagrin.

When Holly became a teenager, Madeline was put to the ultimate test. Holly distanced herself from her mother, as all teenagers do, and she also became very close to her grandmother. It was obvious to everyone that Holly and her grandma were cut from the same cloth: they were social creatures who liked the finer things in life. All Madeline's good intentions, and her vow not to set an agenda, went by the wayside as Holly neared college age and her grades slogged along at C level. Madeline was convinced that without a degree from a top-notch university, Holly would end up checking groceries at the 7-Eleven. She criticized her daughter, nagged her, and eventually became very unpleasant. The fallout from those years lasted a long time, until Holly—grown and married to a successful businessman—convinced her mother to come to counseling.

There was a lot of pain in the room when those two first came to see me. Holly accused her mother of being disappointed in her. "You just don't like who I am," she said, her voice shaking with hurt. Her daughter's anguish was so intense that it pulled Madeline right back to her own girlhood. That was exactly what she had felt about *her* mother. As much as Madeline had tried to avoid her mother's mistakes, she had ended up in the same place by not accepting her daughter's differences.

I urge every woman reading this book to search her memory for trouble spots with her mother. Follow the course of events that began with those trouble spots, and trace the effect they had on the way you raised your daughter. If she and you have similar temperaments, the new route you charted may have worked out perfectly. But if her temperament is fundamentally different than yours, your efforts may have misfired. "I gave her all the opportunities I never had!" mothers commonly complain. Sometimes that's a good thing, but sometimes it's a cause of bitterness and misunderstanding between mother and daughter.

Mother Truths

"My daughter, who is thirty-seven, gets furious with me if I don't approve of her," one exasperated mother told me. "Why do I have to bless her every action?"

Craving Mother's approval is almost a primal urge. Her opinion carries more weight than anyone else's because it was Mom who first introduced us to life—she was our world when we were infants, and as we grew she taught us right from wrong, the frosting from the cake. I have a name for the opinions and values our mothers impressed on us: "mother truths." Mother truths are true beyond reason; they have a soul-deep authority that stays with us forever.

Mother truths can be simple—"Carrots improve your eyesight"—or profound—"Treat others as you would like to be treated," "Never tell a lie," "Don't be wasteful." Sometimes mother truths are obviously inane, but even then we have a hard time shaking them. Marisa, sixty-one, recalled how her mother warned her against masturbating: "If you touch yourself down there, you'll never be able to have babies!" When Marisa was twenty-four, her first child was stillborn. Her mother's threat haunted her like a curse, defying all logic.

Mother truths echo loudest in mother's area of expertise: childrearing, family traditions, principles, and values. Mothers teach us the basic code of civilized behavior. In most families, they are the unwavering moral compass to which the children look for guidance. Even if Dad is an honest and admirable man, chances are he isn't often around to referee the petty clashes over fairness and truth telling that shape a child's moral character.

The value system Mother taught was the most enduring part of her legacy. One of the most important parts of that value system had to do with our attitudes toward men and sexuality. But our mothers' strict moral standards, which most of us rigidly adhered to and planned to pass on to our daughters, were blown out of the water by the sexual revolution of the 1960s.

Of Mothers and Men

For centuries it has been the mother's duty to usher her girl through adolescence into womanhood and protect her until she weds a suitable husband. Until very recently, reputation and marriage meant everything to a woman's future.

But in the mid-1960s, a thunderbolt struck the sexual landscape and made much of our mothers' advice passé. It was the birth control pill, the ticket to sexual freedom for women. Our mothers' admonitions about reputation, virginity, and high moral standards flew by the wayside. Our daughters weren't buying. This was a crucial moment for mothers and daughters, and some of them never recovered from the sexual battles that raged in the 1960s and '70s.

Women of my generation were raised to respect their parents, and *respect* meant *obey*. My mother had only to shoot me a stern look and it was enough to curb my behavior. When it came to boys, everything revolved around maintaining your reputation. In the old country (Spain on my father's side, Latvia on my mother's), a daughter's actions reflected on her family's good name. The village was full of gossips; there were prying eyes everywhere, eager to spot loose behavior in a girl. When parents such as mine emigrated to America, they expected their daughters to uphold these traditional standards. If a girl strayed, her mother might say, "Don't you respect yourself?" What she really meant was, "Don't you respect your parents? You are shaming us by your actions." To women like me, this was a serious, painful transgression.

The 1960s and the Pill changed everything. Our daughters were free in a way we never could have imagined. Some moms envied their daughters' freedom, and this led to tension between them. Other mothers were frankly appalled at their daughters' blooming, blatant sexuality; it made them uncomfortable and embarrassed. In my own family there was a gulf between my daughters and me that hadn't existed between me and my mother. When my mother had warned me, "Be a good girl," I knew exactly what she meant: don't be a tramp. When I'd tell one of my daughters, "Be a good girl," she'd say, "I am! I don't steal, I don't lie, I'm not cruel to people. What does sex have to do with goodness?"

The same scenes that unfolded in my house were unfolding everywhere across the country. We mothers could not control our daughters' sexuality the way our parents had controlled ours. We had to learn to adjust to their new freedom or risk them shutting us out of their lives. Considering how volatile the social climate was at the time and how unsafe the world seemed, many mothers were loath to close down the lines of communication. As we struggled to find a way to understand our daughters, if not approve of them, we hid their actions from our own mothers. They'd never comprehend why we let our daughters "run wild." Grandma would be appalled, so we kept secrets.

Now, thirty-five years after the sexual revolution, it's useful to look back on the adjustments we made to keep our relationship with our daughters afloat. If you were lucky enough to weather those storms, it might be because you were more flexible and open-minded back then, when your daughter was still a babe in the woods who clearly needed your support. The flexibility that helped keep the two of you talking during those years might come in handy today as you try to improve your relationship.

Eventually, our free-spirited daughters usually got married and settled down. We related to them differently once they were married, again taking our cues from the way our mothers treated us once we had found our mates.

Mom as Marriage Counselor

Susanna, fifty-five, came to see me because she was distraught about her daughter Cara's marriage. "I think they're headed for divorce," she told me, and said that she had been calling Cara daily to console her and give her advice. Then, without warning, Cara had informed Susanna that she only wanted to speak to her twice a month, and that she wouldn't discuss her husband anymore. "You're ruining my marriage," she bluntly told her mother.

"Why is it my fault?" Susanna asked me. "She needs someone to talk to."

"Maybe *you* need someone to talk to," I responded gently, "and I think Cara is wise beyond her years." I then asked Susanna to describe the lessons her own mother had taught her about men.

"My father was a saint," Susanna began.

> At least, that's what my mother told me. I don't remember much about him because I was only six when he died. But according to my mother, he was kind and generous and brilliant. She never remarried and always spoke about him in the most glowing terms. In fact, she never had a harsh word about anyone.

Nor did Susanna's mother have a harsh life: Her father had left them a comfortable inheritance, and Susanna lived a sheltered existence until she got married at nineteen.

As it turned out, she should have waited. She married too young to realize that the dashing fellow who swept her off her feet was not the best husband material. Their marriage lurched along for fifteen years, and three kids later ended in an acrimonious divorce. "My mother didn't prepare me for the real world," Susanna said bleakly. "She didn't do me any favor by sparing me the truth. Most men are far from saintlike."

Susanna's perspective on Cara's marriage was clouded not only by her own divorce but by her belief that her mother had misled her. Her mother's legacy had been a positive but somewhat unrealistic view of men, and Susanna was adamant that Cara hear "the truth." But Susanna's truth was as biased as her own mother's view had been.

If you want to share a marital coping strategy with your daughter every now and then, that's fine. But 99 percent of the time, acting as her marriage counselor will backfire—*even if she asks for your help.* If your daughter patches things up with her husband, she'll resent you for knowing their darker secrets. If the marriage fails, she'll resent the part you played in its demise. Your advice is bound to be colored by your own experiences and your mother's legacy, neither of which may be relevant to your daughter's situation. You can't be objective, and you don't have professional counseling skills. So don't do it. Unless your daughter's husband is abusing her, quit your counseling position and return to being a mother.

You Can Marry a Rich Man as Easily as a Poor Man, and Other Dumb Advice

Many of our mothers did not paint a particularly rosy picture of husbands and marriage. Their legacy consisted of dire predictions, warnings, or baffling instructions about how to catch a wealthy man. Sometimes, though, these negative or perplexing messages can spur a positive reaction in the daughter. Irene's story is a good case in point.

"My mother was determined that I not repeat her mistakes," she said.

> She used to chant to me, almost like a mantra: "Don't marry young, like I did." Or "Marry within our religion." One of her favorites was "Never marry a poor man." I had

these chants running through my head and they caused a lot of confusion. For you see, my mother had married at seventeen to a poor man who was not of our religion. He was my beloved father, the nurturing parent in my life, and I was not supposed to marry anyone like him.

Irene's mother had defied her parents when she wed Irene's father in 1925. She was cast out by her family and battled poverty for many years. She wanted desperately to save Irene that heartache, hence her "practical" advice about men. But instead of helping, her mother's warnings deeply wounded and confused Irene, who adored her father.

When Irene became a mother, one of her "nevers" was "I'll never criticize or belittle my husband in front of my children." She restrained herself from judging her daughters' boyfriends too harshly, and taught her girls to focus more on a man's character than the size of his wallet. It didn't insure that her daughters would all enjoy blissful marriages, but Irene felt at peace with her decision.

I Bought Her the House— the Least She Can Do Is Keep It Clean!

There is more to being a mother than any job description can cover. In addition to interacting with the kids, most of us were taught that Mom is also responsible for running the house. At her side we learned to master the details of cooking, cleaning, and entertaining. By the time we got the chance to run our own homes—during the 1950s–1970s, for most of us—good house-keeping had become a near religion. A clean house actually became a standard of character.

Well, times have changed. Pride comes from elsewhere now.

Before the 1980s, a working mother was the exception; nowadays she's the norm. When a woman works full-time, she doesn't generally want to spend the few remaining hours of her day cleaning her house. She may *wish* she could do it, but real life intervenes. What about her husband and kids? Her friends? They deserve her attention as much as the kitchen floor does. Today's women must prioritize their tasks, and housekeeping often ends up at the bottom of the list.

Unless the health department needs to be called in, I usually side with the daughters on this one. I've had way too many encounters with "nutsy clean" moms and their white-glove, hotel standards. The following is typical of the conversations that take place when such a woman walks into her daughter's house.

MOTHER: Boy, this place is loaded.
DAUGHTER: Hello, Mom.
MOTHER: I mean, how can you even get across the room? Look! Your cabinets are overflowing!
DAUGHTER: Forget it, Mom. Leave me alone. I don't have time to organize things your way. This is the way I am.
MOTHER: Well, this is not the way I raised you to be. What happened to you?

Does this dialogue sound familiar? If so, let me invite you to play a little game. Pretend that the house you're entering isn't your daughter's home, but that of a friend. Would you advise her about her housekeeping? Would you say, "Wow, what a messy house! Why don't you put some of this stuff away?" Not if you wanted to keep her friendship, you wouldn't. It's just as rude to criticize your daughter's housekeeping.

Certain mothers seem especially anguished about their daughters' sloppiness. These are the "professional moms" who reveled in their role and did a spectacular job of it. "If a well-run house means so little to my daughter," they wonder, "what does it say about her opinion of me? Does my daughter think I wasted my life taking care of my family?" Most of the time, the answer is no. Your daughter's housekeeping reflects her temperament and schedule; it's not some sort of veiled criticism or reflection of you.

One of the fastest, easiest things you can do to improve your relationship with your daughter is to respect her in her own home and hold your tongue when you visit there. It may be difficult, but give it a try. Those of you who are really determined to change might even announce your plans to your daughter: "Honey, I've decided that what you do with your house is your own business. From now on, you won't hear a word from me about it." Saying it out loud will take the pressure off her and help you keep your word.

Mom's Changing for the Better

As everyone reading this book surely knows, you're never too old to grow. Mothers can bloom after their kids leave the nest, and elderly parents can continue to learn and change. If your mother does this, she is giving you a most valuable legacy.

When I was thirty-two, my husband and I bought our first house in Tonawanda, New York. I thought it was pretty great to own a house, even if the yard was a bare plot of dirt. A few weeks after we moved in, my mother arrived to lend a hand. She was fifty-two then, and all her children were grown and gone. Mother took one look at that bleak backyard and said, "What's going on here? Where's the grass? Where are the kids going to play?"

"We don't have the money to hire a gardener," I replied.

"You're not going to wait for that, are you?" she asked. The next day she was out in the yard with a rented rototiller, breaking up the dirt clumps. She organized my friends and me, and we hauled in fertilizer and seed. In a few weeks, we had a lovely grassy lawn.

My mother had always been industrious, but when we were growing up our large family had burned up every watt of her energy. Once we were out of the house, she began to shine again. My workhorse mother turned into a fun-loving, happy-go-lucky lady who played bridge, took trips, went dancing at night, and always had enough energy to spare for visits to us.

Maybe you don't comprehend your elderly mother's enthusiasm for lawn bowling or duplicate bridge. Maybe you're taken aback by some of the friends she's made at the senior center or are bored by the intrigues of the octogenarian set. But if she's active and interested in the world, take a page from her book. Your mother's independence sends a loud, clear message you can pass on to your daughter: I have continued to change since I finished raising you. I am not just a mother; I am a person.

Exit Laughing

My mother, who stayed vital and involved for most of her life, was somewhat unusual. Often, the women I counsel tell me that their elderly mothers are filled with bitterness and rage. They do not go gently, but instead get crabbier and nastier with each passing year. Yet even if your mother is not a model of grace at this point in her life, there is a lot you can learn from her.

If visiting your elderly mother has become a dreaded chore, ask yourself why. "She complains all the time" is the typical answer. Elderly ladies living in nursing homes complain about the staff, the food, the boredom, the other patients, their children, and of course their aches and pains. As their health deteriorates, their rage intensifies. "I can't believe I'm dying like this," they may say. Or, as one older friend used to put it, "A tree shouldn't grow too close to heaven. Why am I still alive?"

All of this is very frightening to watch. For many old people, negativity seems almost to become a life force, the only thing that keeps them going. Learn from these elders who complain all day and whom no one wants to visit. Foster a positive attitude now, while you're still independent. In your church or synagogue, in your neighborhood, at the market, train yourself to be amiable and interesting. Join a discussion group, start walking every day, get active in local politics. If you miss mothering someone, read to kids in the library or rock babies in the hospital. Whatever you do, get involved with people in a positive way. You may have to make a conscious effort that feels awkward at first, but you must try. Don't let yourself become a negative, complaining old woman.

I sometimes see the seeds of negativity sprouting in clients who are still in their sixties. "I have nothing in common with my daughter," they moan. "If we're not talking about the kids, we have nothing to say." Right now, before you start the long slide into permanent discontent, *develop something in common with your daughter.* Find out what she's reading, and read the same books. Watch the same TV shows. If she's knitting, give it a try yourself. If you know she's planting a particular type of garden, be on the lookout for books, magazines, or TV shows that relate to it, or buy her some plants. If she's involved with a volunteer group, call them up—maybe you can help, too. You have the time, you have the desire to bond with your daughter, so you must be the one to take these extra steps.

Many women live into their eighties and nineties nowadays. If you teach yourself to be upbeat, to be well versed in a few of your daughter's interests, and to cultivate your own hobbies, your kids and grandkids will look forward to visiting you no matter what your age. If you eventually find yourself in a retirement home, your positive attitude and ability to find common ground with others will be invaluable there as well. You can do crafts, become a foster grandparent, start dancing again.

In every nursing home, there are one or two patients who make it their duty to care for the others. True to character, my mother was one of these. Each day she would visit the other patients, asking about their health, their children, their favorite talk show. She'd always connect physically, too—a pat on the shoulder, a squeeze of the hand. Even when her mind started to dim and she became forgetful, she continued to make these daily rounds. I can see her now, seated at a friend's bedside—two frail little ladies holding hands and teasing a favorite nurse about her punk hairdo. My mother's generous spirit was her priceless legacy to me, and I know I have passed it on to my children, all five of them. You can too.

CHAPTER THREE

So, What Did You Expect?

I always thought my kids would want to spend every Sunday with me once they were all grown and out of the house. I thought Sunday dinner was sacrosanct, a time reserved for family. Wrong. Sunday is Scout Jamboree day, ballet recital day, obedience training for the dog day. I tag along sometimes just to make contact, but I usually feel like I'm in the way. We do get together on holidays and birthdays, and I truly appreciate those times. But is this the best I can expect?

—Thelma, age sixty-three

*F*OR ALL THE COMPLEXITY OF MOTHER–DAUGHTER RELAtionships, a single theme runs through every situation: unmet expectations. Mom expects her daughter to be a reincarnation of herself, a younger version who should behave exactly as Mom behaved. Daughter expects Mother to encourage her individuality, but at the same time to approve of all her decisions and be there to nurture her throughout her life. Mother and Daughter each expects the other to *understand* her as if, because they share the same genes, they also share an invisible mind link. Mother and

Daughter both are deeply disappointed in the other's failure to meet her expectations.

Some of the mothers I counsel openly admit that they're sorry they became a parent. They say they'd like to be a grandma and skip the parenting bit—that's how disappointing the child-rearing experience has been for them. When I ask, "What is it that's making you so unhappy?" they say, "My daughter is unavailable. I thought we'd be friends when she grew up; instead, we hardly ever see each other. She doesn't give me any pleasure. I want companionship. I did everything for my daughter that my mother did for me, and I expected her to want to please me, the way I wanted to please my mother."

Why are our daughters so different from us, and is there a way to bridge those differences and leave behind some of the resentment? In most cases, yes. As you read this chapter, you'll probably be surprised to learn how much you have in common with other mothers your age. The disappointments you feel are not unusual; they're the product of a major shift in our society and, especially, the changing roles of women.

Your Daughter Is Not Like You

You know it intellectually, but deep down, do you really accept it? We should delight in our daughters' uniqueness, but instead we often stay stuck in our fantasy of our perfect offspring, our little clone.

"I brought her up," fumed Mary, sixty-eight, after another catch-as-catch-can meal at her daughter's house. "She lived with me. Why doesn't she set a table with china? Why does she use paper plates?" *Why isn't she like me?* is what Mary really means. Mothers such as she cannot believe that after they devoted the best years of their lives to training their daughters, the daughters insist on doing things their own way. "She's got the china I bought her. She's got a dishwasher. She knows it would make me happy. Why can't she just do it?" asks Mary. But rather than trying to please their moms, as women of my generation did, our daughters say, "I wasn't put on this earth to please you. I have to do things my own way."

Those words hurt, but they shouldn't. It's not such a harsh truth, after all. Our daughters were *not* put on this earth to please us. They were not given to us to fulfill our expectations.

When a mom comes to see me the first time, she's often full of confusing, unexamined anger that tends to get vented at a target such as paper plates. Those hot spots are just symbols of the larger problem. To get an accurate look at the big picture, I ask moms to take a legal-size sheet of paper and catalog every single expectation they had concerning their daughter. After each expectation, I have them describe how things actually turned out. In this way, we're able to pinpoint the specific issues that are undermining Mom's relationship with her daughter and review them in a productive manner.

Take the time now to compile your own list. Write down all your expectations and every disappointment you feel toward your daughter, no matter how petty. You will never show this list to anyone, especially her. In fact, my advice is to destroy the list when you're through doing the work in this chapter! The last thing you want is for your daughter to discover it some day, after the two of you are on better terms.

The questions on the next page will get you started, but feel free to add anything that occurs to you. Vent to your heart's content. Later you'll prioritize your problems with your daughter and come up with a set of goals for your relationship.

If You Had Three Wishes . . .

That exercise might have been somewhat emotionally exhausting. If so, take a break—go brew yourself a cup of tea or coffee. As you sip, review your list of expectations and disappointments.

[EXERCISE]
The Confidential List of
Expectations and Disappointments

- How did you expect your daughter to honor you?
- How did you expect your daughter to give you pleasure?
- How did you expect your daughter to make you proud of her?
- Did you expect your daughter to go to college?
- Did you expect your daughter to marry?
- Did you expect your daughter to raise a family?
- How often did you expect to have contact with your daughter?
- What role did you expect to play in your daughter's extended family?
- What did you expect your daughter's personality to be like?
- Do you see yourself in your daughter? Does she look like you? Does she act like you?
- How did you expect your daughter to look?
- How do you feel about your daughter's weight?
- Is your daughter a feminist? If so, do you understand her views on women's roles?
- How do you feel about your daughter's marriage?
- How do you feel about your daughter's divorce?
- How do you feel about your daughter's abortion?
- How do you feel about your daughter's neglect of you?
- How do you feel about the way your grandchildren are being raised?
- How do you feel about your daughter not marrying?
- How do you feel about the fact that your daughter has decided to have a child out of wedlock?
- How do you feel about your daughter being a lesbian?
- How do you feel about your daughter's criticism of you?

Some of the minor grievances will probably seem funny, while other more serious problems will hit home hard. Writing this list is crucial to succeeding with the program in this book; you must know what you're dealing with as you begin this rebuilding project. You are up against your fantasy daughter, that lithe, sweet, devoted creature you created out of your expectations.

After you've looked over your list, begin the weeding-out process. Your goal is to identify the top three problems that are really damaging your relationship. First, strike out the petty irritations that you can live with, for example, your daughter serving dinner on paper plates, or always arriving late, or dressing her kids like welfare recipients.

When you've crossed out the small stuff, turn your attention to disappointments from the past that cannot be changed: abortions, divorces, bankruptcy, DUIs, repossessed cars, the size six your daughter wore when she was in college that has ballooned to a size sixteen. See if you can let go of these failings and forgive her—if not now, perhaps later on in the process. Realize too that no matter how disappointed you may be in your daughter, the unhappy events in her life hurt her more than they hurt you, even if she acted nonchalant about them at the time. If you were vocal about your disapproval, that only added to her anguish. Try now to bury your criticisms once and for all. Criticism, resentment, and judgments won't change your daughter anyway; they'll only undermine your progress with her.

At this point you should be left with a list of serious problems that are taking place in the present. You need to pick three as the areas that you most want to improve on. As you scan your list of problems, you may be overwhelmed with feelings of despair or anger. How can you hone in on just three, when all of them feel painful?

Begin by chosing the problems that hurt the most—the ones that keep you awake at night. Even if an item seems relatively petty, if it's still on the list, pay attention to it. Is this a problem you complain about to your friends? Does it gnaw at you, or pop into your mind at unusual moments? Does thinking about this problem fill you with anxiety that seems out of proportion to the facts of the matter? Dig deeper, and you may discover why.

Moira, fifty-four, was incensed that her thirty-year-old daughter still brought her dirty laundry over for Moira to wash. I suggested that Moira simply stop playing washer woman, and within days, she did. But it wasn't just a matter of unsaddling herself from a dreary task. Several weeks after Moira had washed her last load of clothes, the laundry turned up on her list.

"Why does it still bother me?" Moira questioned.

"Well, think about it," I responded. "You usually give your dirty laundry to someone who's lesser than you; you give it to a maid. It's an insult." On Moira's top-three list, she crossed out "I resent having to do my daughter's laundry" and replaced it with "I wish my daughter would treat me with respect."

Seemingly minor problems that burn a hole in your sleep are usually symptoms of a larger issue. Think about the items on your list, and ask yourself what issues they represent. The list below includes the issues raised most frequently by my clients, but it is by no means all-inclusive.

I Wish My Daughter . . .

- would stop asking me for money
- were not so envious of me
- treated me with respect
- included me in more of her activities
- didn't resent my new husband
- would take my advice more seriously
- enjoyed my company
- would stop blaming me for her problems
- would stop ganging up on me with her siblings
- would stop vying with me for her father's attention
- were not so angry at me
- weren't so judgmental

- didn't make fun of me, especially in front of others
- had more in common with me
- were not so dependent on me
- were not so independent; it seems as if she doesn't need me
- were not so superficial
- didn't resent me
- called and visited me more often
- were not so competitive with me
- would stop complaining

Your three most urgent problems will become part of the wish list you'll use as a blueprint to repair your relationship. The rest of the wish list can be culled from a basic set of standards I've created to give moms an idea of what comprises a normal relationship. In the following section, I spell out these "reasonable expectations." Lord knows we can't count on other mothers to help us define *reasonable*. According to most of our friends and relatives, their daughters are beyond reproach—only ours are a challenge.

The Reasonably Good Daughter

If you have a difficult daughter, you may have been trying for years to figure out exactly what a good daughter is. You had your expectations, which she didn't meet. But how did she compare to your friends' daughters? Your sister's? Your coworkers'? Chances are you never found out because, quite frankly, mothers fib. They don't admit when their daughters are neglecting or exploiting them, and they embellish their daughters' achievements. Everyone tries to save face and hide the negative aspects of her relationship.

Mothers fib to one another because we are social creatures constantly comparing ourselves to our peers. If our daughter visits us once a month but Mrs. Pierson across the street gets weekly visits, it bothers us. Her daughter seems more devoted, better. This compare-and-contrast game is rampant among mothers. With the territory goes exaggerating our daughter's successes, her husband's earnings, her children's grades or baseball scores, and on and on.

But we moms can't lie to ourselves. We want to have a good daughter, and we'd dearly love to know how close we are to that goal. To help mothers and daughters work out their relationships, I've devised the list below, which outlines what I believe a mother can reasonably expect from a daughter. Please, resist the urge to wave this list in your daughter's face. It's not a mandate; it's just a guideline.

Reasonable Expectations

- Contact once a week, by phone or in person. Contact can be initiated by either mother or daughter.
- A verbal or written thank-you for gifts or baby-sitting.
- A visit at least once a month, if mother and daughter live in the same city.
- An offer to drive Mother to the hospital or doctor's office if serious medical tests are required and the doctor suggests Mom be driven home (if at all possible given the daughter's schedule).
- A query as to the result of any serious medical test.
- An offer to drive Mother to or from the airport if it does not interfere with Daughter's work schedule.
- Participation in a holiday celebration at least once or twice a year.
- Periodic visits from an out-of-town daughter, depending on distance and financial concerns.
- A card on Mother's Day and on Mom's birthday. If the family has a tradition of gift giving, Mom should get a gift on these occasions as well.
- A party for special birthdays.
- Open, direct communication from the daughter as to what pleases or displeases her.

From this list of basics, choose those that are important to you. Some items may not apply—perhaps you don't really mind if your daughter visits only once every other month, or maybe your husband is available to drive you to the doctor. Trim the list to suit your own needs, but don't expect any *more* of your daughter than the list suggests.

When you've assembled your personalized reasonable-expectations list, add to it the three problems you chose to focus on in the previous section. This combined list is your wish list. As you read this book, keep your wish list in mind when deciding which courses of action to follow. It's especially important to review the wish list when you're choosing which battles to fight and which to let go of. If you stay focused on the goals in the wish list, you'll see results much sooner.

My Daughter in All Her Glory

Before you spend too much time obsessing on your daughter's drawbacks, it's only fair to give her her due. Take a few moments now to concentrate on your daughter's positive attributes—after all, we are rebuilding your relationship, not tearing it down. On another sheet of paper, write down all the good things about your daughter, not only as she relates to you but in her life outside of your relationship. Be generous, appreciative, and complimentary. The list below is taken from my clients—perhaps it will inspire you.

My Daughter Is a Great . . .

- Mother. Her kids are turning out beautifully.
- Career woman. She's earned many promotions and has an impressive job.
- Animal lover and pet rescuer.
- Volunteer. She enjoys helping those less fortunate than she.

- Homemaker. She sets a great table and creates a warm environment.
- Children's chauffeur—and she stays good-natured about it.
- Juggler. I could never handle the amount of work she does plus a family, but I admire her ability to do it.
- Wife. Her husband is very happy with her and treats her well.
- Party planner and organizer. She's always the one to gather the family together and make sure everyone is taken care of.
- Cook. Even if it's instant Jell-O, it always tastes wonderful.
- Joke teller and entertainer.
- Gardener. Her vegetables would win prizes at the county fair.
- Exerciser. She runs more miles in a week than I drive.
- Fund-raiser. She's raised more money for her kids' school than any other mom.
- Friend. She's always there to help her friends in need, and she has lots of friends.

Okay, those were easy. All of the above attributes are clearly positive. But what about reframing some of the things that are not so wonderful, things that bother you about your daughter? Let's try turning negatives into positives. Here's what I mean.

My Daughter Is a Wonderful . . .

- Debater. She could argue anybody into the ground, and that takes skill.
- Excuse maker. Talk about creativity—she should have been a writer.
- Systems analyst. She knows all the systems: Welfare, Medicaid, SSI . . .
- Procrastinator. Her delays are an art form.
- Bargain hunter. She could get a Ph.D. in smart shopping.

- Eccentric. She's a thrift-store maven, a bizarre but beautiful dresser.
- Comedian. Instead of dealing with truths she does a routine—but she sure is funny.
- Amateur doctor. She knows every ailment in the book, and all the latest treatments.
- Dietitian. If you need to know the calorie count in a grape, call her up.
- Collector. Her house is full of fascinating odds and ends.

The idea isn't to create a list of backhanded compliments, but to try to appreciate some of the quirks that might normally irritate you. There's certainly some good-hearted humor in a list like this, but that doesn't mean it's insincere. It's merely a new way of looking at things.

The list of your daughter's positive attributes is one you should keep. Give her a copy at an appropriate time, for instance, tucked into a birthday card. Or use the list to break the ice, as a peace offering when you begin initiating the changes in your relationship.

Now that you have composed your wish list and reminded yourself of your daughter's good points, you're almost ready to embark on the main leg of the journey—fixing the bond with your dependent, dissatisfied, or distant daughter. Before you set off, however, you need to be aware of the other side of the equation: your daughter's expectations.

What Do Daughters Want?

I don't know your daughter, but I know a few things about her. I know what she wants.

She wants your approval if possible, but at the very least, your acceptance. She wants you to recognize that she is an individual, not an extension of you. She wants you to stop criticizing her. She wants you to mother her. She wants your love and nurturance; sometimes she wants your sympathy.

Most mothers are capable of providing all of the above. It's just a matter of deciding *how* you're going to provide it—what boundaries you're comfortable with, what gifts you want to give, what amount of nurturing you feel you can offer. You must figure out your place in your daughter's life, and her place in yours, and then you can try to give her what she needs.

The most important thing for you to understand, and the foundation of everything you will learn in this book, is that your daughter is an individual. She's not part of you anymore, *but she is not against you.* Just because she doesn't do things your way doesn't mean she's your enemy. She's just being herself. If you can be big enough and bold enough to put aside your unrealistic expectations and say, "Wow, isn't she unique!" the two of you can walk side by side and establish a beautiful, adult relationship.

The psychological term for daughters growing up and separating from their mothers is *differentiation.* Some daughters who don't fully differentiate become dependent on their mothers; others become the dissatisfied girls who can't let a day go by without logging an hour of complaint time on the phone with Mom. But there is another side to differentiation—the mother's side. Many of the mothers I counsel can't draw the line between "she" and "I." This is the root of their problem with their daughters—they do not differentiate from them.

As we saw in chapter one, until quite recently the psychiatric community held Mom responsible for her daughter's character and actions. This feeds into Mom's instinctive desire to control her daughter and shape her destiny. If all goes well, Mom can then take credit for her daughter's successes (an entirely inappropriate response—your daughter's successes are hers, not yours). But when a daughter falls short of her mother's expectations, the differentiation issue becomes lethal. All those disappointments you listed a few pages back are due to the fact that your daughter didn't behave the way you would have behaved. Guess what? She probably never will.

When your girl was growing up, you had a duty to teach her values and standards of decent, civilized behavior. Now that she is an adult, you no longer have that duty or that right. You don't have the right to comment on her weight, clothing, or hairstyle. You don't have the right to criticize her choice of companions. Unless she is harming her children, you don't have the right to comment on her method of child rearing. The good news is that you're not responsible for her, either. You are off the hook, so let her off the hook. If she asks for your opinion, you are certainly entitled to give it truthfully, but measure that honesty with discretion and tact. If she doesn't ask your opinion, don't offer. No one likes unsolicited advice, and it doesn't usually change people anyway. They listen and then go ahead and do as they please.

Whenever I start complaining too heatedly about one of my grown daughters, my husband Simon has a wonderful retort: "It's not your movie." Your daughter is living in her movie, the one she wrote, produced, and directed. You are living in your movie. They are playing in adjacent theaters, but they are not the same film. Accept this, and you will take a giant leap forward in your relationship with your daughter.

Aim for Acceptance and Compassion Rather than Approval and Understanding

One complaint I often hear from mothers and daughters alike is "She just doesn't understand me." Our daughters expect us to understand them now, when they're thirty or forty, just as we did when they were five. By *understand,* they mean agree with their train of logic, agree that the decision they made was the right one, agree that there were no other options. If we really understood them, they say, we'd approve of them.

We can't always do this, of course. Some of the decisions our daughters make are stupid, shortsighted, and even masochistic. But unless a crime has been committed, we must always *accept* our daughters' choices (then go into the shower stall and scream!). Approval and acceptance are very different animals. Your daughter may want approval, but she'll learn to make do with acceptance. After you've mastered the art of accepting, you can move on to the next level: developing compassion for her no matter how infuriating or puzzling her predicament might be.

"My daughter is a credit-card addict," confided Abby, fifty-nine. "She won't even tell me how much debt she and her husband have run up. Why can't they just control themselves? When I was her age, I paid off those credit cards every single month. And we had a mortgage. And we had savings. She needs to learn how to handle money."

The debt debate tends to bring out the worst in mothers, and it's a good example of the lack of compassion I sometimes see in older moms. When it comes to finances, these moms judge their kids according to the rules that existed in the 1950s and '60s, when they were raising their own families. Although it's common knowledge that the standard of living has dropped since then and it takes two salaries to support most households, some mothers show little empathy for their daughters' situations. Instead, it's "Why can't she do it like I did?" She can't do it your way because she's living in the 1990s, not the 1960s.

Without auditing her bank account and monthly bills, you'll probably never really understand why your daughter is in debt. But you can try not to judge her so harshly; you can give her the benefit of the doubt. You might even consider giving her a monetary gift—not a loan—to ease her burden, if it won't be a strain on you. (Loaning money can make your relationship worse if your daughter will have a hard time repaying you.) Even if you can't help her out financially, you can empathize with her. She needs that more than a lecture on economizing.

Formulas for Access to Your Daughter

"She wouldn't pick me up at the airport!" mothers commonly complain. "She only visited for an hour." "I never get a chance to see her alone." Nearly every mom wants her adult daughter to be more of a friend. Mothers feel entitled to this friendship, but their daughters always seem to be working, or rushing off to pick up the kids, or going to exercise class. Moms often feel like they're last on the to-do list, and that stings. But how do our daughters view the situation?

"My life is too full," explains Dianne, thirty-four. "I'm overwhelmed."

> I'd love to spend more time with my mother, especially since our visits are relatively relaxing—we go out to lunch or go shopping together. It's playtime. What she doesn't understand is that I've got a dozen other balls in the air, from the kids, to my job, to making sure my husband doesn't feel completely left out of my life. So when I do spend time with Mom and she ends up complaining that it's not *enough* time, I want to strangle her. "There are close friends I haven't talked to in months!" I want to shout. "I'm giving you all I can. Please, please accept that gracefully."

Mothers love to tsk-tsk over their daughters' heavy schedules and to critique their priorities. "Why do her kids have so many structured activities?" is a typical question. "My kids just played together on the block. It's better that way—they get to be more creative." Again the answer is that we live in a different world than the one that existed thirty years ago. Like it or not, it's a more dangerous world. Playing on the block isn't such a great idea in many parts of town, and there are fewer at-home parents to keep an eye on those twilight games of hide-and-seek. Most parents are at the office until five or six each night, and when they do get home they have to launch right into the dinner-homework-bath relay.

All of this translates into an explosion of work for today's young mother. She's the one who generally arranges the transportation to the children's activities. She still does the bulk of the shopping, errands, cooking, and cleaning, in addition to working at an outside job. The result: Your daughter is tired and tense. What she needs from her mom is an offer of help, not a complaint. The good part is, you can get what you want—more time with your daughter—by giving her what she wants. The key word is *giving*. Offering to help your daughter will instantly make you more involved in her life.

In truth, many moms criticize their daughters' heavy schedules because the schedules don't include Mom. But Mom doesn't want to spend just any old time with her daughter—she wants quality time. She wants to go shopping, go for a leisurely brunch, take in a movie. If you insist on quality time, you'll get it, but not often. Learn to enjoy those special afternoons or evenings and don't pressure your daughter for more. Instead, develop interests of your own. Reinvent yourself rather than trying to change your daughter.

If, on the other hand, you change your attitude and offer to help with the nitty-gritty, not-so-leisurely details of your daughter's life, you'll suddenly find yourself much more involved with her and her family. For instance, most older moms wait to be asked to baby-sit the grandkids. Instead of waiting, offer. Ask your daughter how you can help ease her burden. Offer to drive her carpool one day a week or do her marketing for her. Pick up her cleaning. Pick up the kids from Little League once in a while. Cook her family a meal (or buy take-out) and bring it over, all ready for the table that you set for her. Remember, it's a lot easier for her if you bring a meal rather than extend an invitation to your house, because it saves her from having to organize and transport the kids. A simple casserole at her place will probably please her as much as an elaborate feast at yours.

Offer to baby-sit for a weekend so your daughter can have a birthday away. I know you'd rather be there with her, with the cake and candles and a party, but maybe she needs a break. Focus on her needs instead of yours. Ask your daughter to make a list of chores you could help with. You don't have to do everything she asks, but she'll probably be pleased and grateful for any help she gets. Folding a load of clothes gives her a few precious moments of breathing room.

And what do you get in return for two or three hours of your time each week? Your daughter's thanks. The great feeling that comes from giving of yourself. More time with your grandkids— casual time, time to get to know them intimately. And you get more time with your daughter because, since you're taking on a few of her tasks, she has more time to spare.

One note of caution: Volunteer to help only if you can do so cheerfully, uncritically, and willingly. Expect nothing in return. Do not attach strings to your offers, and don't expect a payback. The payback is the day-to-day access to your daughter and her family.

You'll Always Be Your Daughter's Mother

At one recent group session, the moms and I spent a good hour chuckling about our daughters' seemingly endless requests. One reason the above tactic—offering to help—is so effective is that it's generous and it cuts your daughter off at the pass. She's proba-bly going to ask you for things anyway, so you might as well be the one who decides what you give.

"My daughter Shana is a professional hinter," said Rosalee.

> **And when she hints, she expects me to *get it*. Sometimes it's money. Sometimes it's my mother's heirloom jewelry—**

she wants it now, not later. Last week it was a trip to San Francisco. She was grumbling about how much the airfare cost, but I played dumb. Why should I buy her an airplane ticket? She earns twice as much as I do, and I never get to go to San Francisco.

Although we had a good laugh about it, the mood sobered when Rosalee asked the question all the moms were thinking:"Why are these girls so needy?"

It's true that some daughters are exceptionally needy. These are usually the dependent daughters, whom we'll discuss in Part II. But many "hinters" are really asking for symbols of their mothers' love. Even the most demanding daughter can be softened if you get there first, with offers of help or tangible tokens of your affection.

These tokens do not have to be expensive because money is not the issue—it's the gesture that counts. A greeting card will do, or a bag of fresh croissants. Buy her a subscription to a magazine. Take her a pound of peaches from the gourmet market. Bring her a pot of spring flowers. Or just call and ask how her day was (and don't criticize her or complain about your own day). You don't have to buy your daughter a leather jacket or a Lexus, but you do have to spend a few minutes shopping for a card or token of your love.

"Well, she never calls me or sends me a card like that," mothers often respond. To that I say, "Aren't we the teachers, by virtue of our age, experience, and wisdom?" You will always be your daughter's mother. She'll always crave your love and acceptance. When your are ninety and she is sixty-five, it'll still be the same. So take the lead, be compassionate, send her a sign that you care. The more regularly you do this, the more you'll see her requests diminish. It's like a countervailing weight. You fill a child up with enough nurturance, affection, love, and symbols of that love, and her neediness will gradually subside.

There is one golden rule to remember about giving: Don't be

manipulative. If you're giving your daughter a gift in order to get something in return, she'll see through your strategy and feel (correctly) that you're trying to control her. So search your heart for your motive before you give.

Sunny, seventy-four, told the group how frustrated she was when her daughter called at the last minute to inform her that her husband would not be able to attend a concert for which Sunny had purchased expensive seats. "She asked me if we could take her six-year-old son instead! I don't want to waste a hundred-dollar seat on a six-year-old," said Sunny. After I asked her a few questions, it became clear that every time Sunny bought tickets for her daughter and son-in-law, some snafu erupted.

"You're missing the message," I suggested. "Your daughter doesn't want those tickets; she just doesn't have the guts to say so. Instead she makes last-minute excuses." By purchasing the tickets without first consulting her daughter, Sunny got to control the visit, plus she got companionship at the theater. For a well-to-do woman like Sunny, the money was no object. After thinking it over, Sunny realized that it would make more sense to consult with her daughter before planning these cultural outings. That way they'd all have a say in the event, and no one would feel inconvenienced or manipulated.

Staging a Mother Revolt

All the things your daughter expects from you—acceptance, compassion, acknowledgment of her individuality, signs of your love—are easy to give if you and she are on good terms. But if things were so terrific between you and your daughter, you wouldn't be reading this book. More likely, the two of you feel a lot of resentment toward each other, if not outright hostility. Sending your daughter roses might be the last thing on earth you feel like doing right now; in fact, you might doubt that you can ever undo all the bad feelings or let go of the pain. But believe me, you can. The bond between mother and daughter is surprisingly resilient. It never completely breaks, no matter how stretched and strained it may be.

Sometimes after an especially painful group session where mothers have recounted their daughters' self-centered, exploitative, or cruel behavior, I end the hour exclaiming, "We need a mother revolt! We're mad as hell and we're not going to take it anymore!" It's true—we do need to revolt against our old ways of interacting with our daughters. We must regain our self-respect and take charge of our own destiny.

We moms must own up to the fact that much of what we had expected of our daughters was a fantasy. We must look at the real women they are today, in all their beauty and imperfection. We must devise realistic goals for our relationships with them, and then we've got to announce loudly and clearly what we expect from them. And everything we expect from our daughters, we must be willing to give them in return. That way, when the dust settles, we can live together as equals and friends.

PART TWO

THE DEPENDENT

DAUGHTER

Joined at the Hip

My daughter called me yesterday to tell me she is pregnant. Ordinarily you'd congratulate me, but under the circumstances, I'm very upset. She moved away years ago and I thought everything was terrific. Now she tells me she wants to come home to have her baby, and that the father was just a casual acquaintance. She sold her business and is packing up her apartment this week. I'm too old for this! I want to help her and I know she needs my help, but who is going to help me?

—Muriel, age sixty-eight

SOME DAUGHTERS JUST CAN'T SEEM TO HOLD A JOB, OR keep a marriage together, or provide a stable home for their children. Over the past decade I've seen a real increase in the dependent-daughter syndrome, as grown women move back in with their parents or, pushed off balance by some crisis, appeal to Mom and Dad for financial help. When a daughter asks for support, few moms have the heart to say no, even though trying to save her is usually a doomed proposition. Not only will you fail but you may also damage your relationship with her, and your marriage may begin to crack under the pressure as well.

Outside observers and relatives are often impatient or incredulous that you've landed in this situation. "She's conning you," your best friend may warn. Your own mother may demand, "What's wrong with her? She has a college degree. Why isn't she working?" Your answer to all of the above probably begins with, *I know, but . . .*

She said it would just be for six months.
She had an awful year and can't seem to get back on her feet.
Her husband left and she's devastated.
She lost her job.
She's pregnant.
She can't find a decent apartment.
She graduated and can't decide what she wants to do next.
Her kids need a good neighborhood.

Each of these is a perfectly sensible excuse, in the beginning. But by the time most mothers of dependent daughters seek my help, the beginning was a long, long while ago. The original crisis that led to the daughter's dependency has faded, and she is now on permanent parental life support. Meanwhile, Mom's vital energy, patience, and funds are strained to the breaking point. The daughter's crisis began the cycle of dependency, but it takes another crisis—Mom's—to put an end to it.

In this chapter we'll explore the many facets of dependency and the reasons mothers and daughters get caught up in this destructive pattern. Once you understand the core emotional ingredients of your dilemma, it will become much easier to start making changes.

I Don't Know Where I End and She Begins

Some moms are very aware that they have a big problem with their dependent daughters; they just don't know how to deal with it. If your daughter, her boyfriend, and their child have been camped out in your master bedroom for three years (the case with one of my clients), there's not much question that things need to change. Other mothers have daughters whose demands have not yet reached the outrageous point but seem to be moving in that direction. These moms feel uneasy with the amount of support they're giving, but don't think they have the right to feel that way.

One of the most pervasive myths of motherhood is that a mom must be there for her daughter—body, soul, and checkbook—for as long as they both shall live. "I can't say no to her," mothers often tell me. For this reason, they may have a hard time recognizing that their daughter has crossed the line into dependency. They don't want to hurt her, and they often enjoy her company, but her neediness seems to be snowballing out of control. Still, they wonder, who can define a normal amount of neediness? Every relationship is different.

In some respects, these moms are right. Although you can get a general idea of an average mother-daughter relationship from the "reasonable expectations" in chapter three, many moms and daughters have a closer bond than the one outlined there. Perhaps they enjoy getting together once a week rather than once a month. Maybe they've set up a schedule where they share child-care duties for the grandkids and see each other every day. That's fine, if both are happy with the arrangement. You should genuinely feel comfortable about the amount of time you spend with your daughter and the amount of support, both financial and emotional, that you give her. *Comfortable*—not guilty, or sorry for her, or afraid to say no to her. If you are experiencing little twinges (or major pangs) of discomfort, it's time to change the regimen. Ask yourself the following questions:

- Does your relationship with your daughter feel oppressive?
- Is it no longer fun to spend so much time with your daughter?

- Are you feeling burdened?
- Are you feeling taken advantage of?
- Do you resent expending so much energy on your daughter and her problems?
- Are you burnt out?
- Does your daughter ask you for more money than you can afford to give her?
- Are you doing without basic services or household necessities in order to help finance your daughter's life?
- Are you afraid to tell your daughter that your money is running out?
- Have you no more free time because your daughter so often demands your opinion, guidance, companionship, and problem-solving abilities?
- Are you afraid to say no to your daughter?
- Are you running out of you—have you and she become one merged soul?
- Do you have a hard time distinguishing who has the problem?

If you answered yes to any of these questions, you need to change some of the ground rules in your relationship. Before you do, it's important to understand the nature of your daughter's dependency and to realize why you've allowed yourself to become her rescuer (or, as they say in twelve-step programs, her enabler). Later on in this chapter we'll take a close look at your rescuing role, but first let's focus on your daughter's dependency.

I've Fallen and I Won't Get Up

The following scenario, although it's as compelling as the best soap opera, has became all too familiar to me. A mother will schedule a session, sit down in my office, and stare at me with a look of utter helplessness or panic. "I don't know how I got into this situation," she'll say. "My daughter has become completely helpless and dependent on me." The details may be different from case to case, but most helpless daughters follow a predictable pattern. Lori's story is a textbook example.

Lori told me that her daughter, once gainfully employed as a medical secretary, had not held a job for four years. Lori and her husband, both in their mid-sixties, had been supporting Rhonda, now twenty-six, all that time. They paid her rent, bought her clothes and food, paid her car payment, bought her gasoline, and in addition to all that gave her a monthly allowance. It all began with a man whom Lori described as "unscrupulous":

> He convinced Rhonda she had a future in dancing. She was only twenty-two then, and had always wanted to dance professionally. She does have talent, and is a very beautiful girl, but before she met this character she hadn't seriously considered dancing as a career. He prodded her to ask for our support, so we gave her dance lessons.
>
> She got a break and was hired for a four-week gypsy chorus job at the Shubert Theater. Well, that was all she needed. Now she asked if we'd support her for a year and pay for more lessons, an agent, a manager, costumes, shoes, photo layouts—you can't imagine what was involved.
>
> At about the same time, Rhonda started seeing a psychologist because she was suffering bouts of mania and depression. When she asked for our help, that is, money, we were afraid to say no. We didn't want to cause her any more emotional problems.
>
> I'm not sorry that we helped Rhonda follow her dream, but I am sorry that she wasn't mentally up to the stresses of being a professional performer. After a year of disappointments, she crashed. Her boyfriend quickly disappeared, of course. Rhonda was briefly hospitalized and has been on medication for depression ever since.

"That was three years ago?" I asked.

"Yes," replied Lori.

"But why hasn't she gotten another job?" I probed.

"She says she's too depressed to look for work. Besides, she's become very eccentric. She's gained a lot of weight and wears flowing robes that make her look like she lives in an ashram. She's got five earrings in one ear, and she's bleached her hair white-blond." At this point, Lori's face crumpled and she started to weep. "Please help me! We can't afford to support her any more. I'm so afraid to refuse her—what will happen to her if we let her down? Maybe she'll end up a street person and we'll never see her again. But if we keep paying for her, *we'll* end up on the street!"

Lori's story had all the elements common to most dependent daughter–rescuing mother (and father) teams. The daughter is functioning well, holding a job, when something happens to throw her off balance. It may be boyfriend problems, getting fired from a job, having a car repossessed, falling behind in her rent, getting pregnant. Her original request may be reasonable, but soon it escalates and she becomes increasingly dependent on her parents. Once she is dependent on them, she starts to develop traits and habits that exacerbate her helplessness. She may become "unhirable" by dint of her odd looks or off-putting personality, or she may lack the confidence to face the job market and chalk it up to depression. Her therapist may even encourage this helplessness (more about your daughter's therapist in chapter six). In the end, the daughter's parents are too frightened for her welfare to cut off the support. An even deeper fear also lurks: they're afraid that if they trim back the aid, she'll get angry and refuse to see them. They're afraid she'll abandon them.

The Eight-Hundred-Pound Gorilla: Are You Really So Helpless?

What kind of grown woman would accept her parents' support for four years? The kind whose parents can *afford* to support her for four years. In my practice I've seen that it's the affluent parents who have the most dependent daughters. It's a matter of supply and demand. If a daughter has been out on her own for a few years and suddenly stumbles, any good mom will extend a hand to see her through the crisis. If Mom lives in a one-bedroom apartment, help might consist of letting her daughter sleep on the couch for a few weeks. Chances are, by that time the daughter will have a pretty stiff neck and be motivated to get on with her life and back into her own apartment.

But if Mom lives in a sprawling home with a nice spare bedroom and fully stocked refrigerator, the daughter's motivation for leaving will plummet. She's already made the big leap—admitting she needs help. Now that she's in helpless mode, she may find it's awfully cozy. Mom feels sorry for her and pampers her; Dad treats her like his precious, long-lost girl. If there are children involved, the stakes are even higher: now she's got in-house baby-sitters, and perhaps a bigger space and nicer yard for the kids. Why should she leave?

When a daughter is not working, the problem takes on much more serious dimensions. Inevitably, future plans are put on hold until she finds a satisfying job with a humane boss, decent pay, and good benefits. Beggars can't be choosers, but the dependent daughter is not a beggar. She can be as choosy as she likes as long as her parents are footing the bills.

Even if a daughter has not moved into her parents' home, I've seen many cases where she will stay financially dependent for years simply because she can. Often, it's not a matter of actually being helpless, it's a matter of being human. Plenty of people don't like to work, or to work hard. Many have not found their niche in life and feel stifled and unhappy in their jobs. It doesn't take a personality disorder to deflate a person's will to work. A brief failure and a too-comfortable safety net are enough to pull many people into dependency.

After years of clinical practice, I've learned that most "helpless" daughters are quite capable of supporting themselves. They've just chosen an easier path—playing on their parents' sympathy. Deep down, most parents of dependent daughters know this is true, but they ignore the obvious. So, as your daughter sits in your living room eating your chicken sandwiches and snuggling into your favorite armchair, it's as if an eight-hundred-pound gorilla were sitting there in the middle of the room too. Everyone walks around it, but no one makes a comment. No one dares ask the question that might humiliate, embarrass, or anger their daughter: "How helpless are you, really?"

Does Your Daughter Have an Emotional Problem?

If you are not a psychiatrist, it can be hard to tell whether your lethargic, unhappy daughter has suffered an emotional collapse or has simply fallen into a pattern of helplessness. Occasionally, a grown woman does develop a psychological condition that leaves her unable to function normally. Below, I've listed some telltale behaviors that would indicate if your daughter is among this small group. If you believe that she is, you must get her to a physician or mental health professional right away, before her illness gets worse or she does something drastic such as attempt suicide.

As I mentioned earlier, most dependent daughters land at their mothers' doorsteps because of a crisis. It's usually a loss of some sort: getting fired from a job; going bankrupt and losing a home; getting divorced; losing a custody battle. Sometimes the loss is physical—the daughter is in a car accident, becomes ill, or is the victim of a crime such as rape or robbery. In some cases the death of a spouse, child, friend, or the other parent has triggered an acute depression. These are grave problems that deserve a parent's sympathy and loving attention. Victims of crime, assault, and sexual or physical abuse need professional help immediately. Do not hesitate: call the police and go to the nearest hospital for aid. Similarly, if your daughter is coping with the death of a loved one, I strongly recommend that she go to a counselor or bereavement group to get help in dealing with her loss.

It's normal for your daughter to have intense emotional reactions to traumas such as these. Some typical reactions are listed below.

Symptoms of Acute Depression

- Staying in bed during the day; insomnia at night
- Unusual eating habits: not eating at all or overeating
- Not bathing or dressing properly; ignoring personal hygiene
- Neglecting the details of everyday life: not paying bills, not answering the doorbell or phone, not returning messages, not locking the door when leaving the house, etc.
- Frequent weeping and lamenting
- Self-medicating: taking alcohol or drugs (either illegal or over-the-counter)
- Making statements such as "I'm no good," "I really don't like myself," "I'm a failure"
- Fabricating peculiar, unrealistic schemes for the future, such as suddenly deciding to become a farmer, airline pilot, or peace corps volunteer
- Showing signs of "agitated depression": unusually high, frenetic energy; nonstop walking, talking, or moving in a way that differs from her normal behavior; sleeplessness and hyperactivity
- Making apathetic statements such as "I don't ever want to leave this house" or "I never want to have a job again"

- Appearing unable to experience pleasure
- Acting lethargic and apathetic; avoiding contact with people

This is only a partial list, and I want to stress that moms must not play lay psychiatrist with their daughters. I've provided these symptoms only to give you a broad idea of the depressed personality, so that you can get your daughter help if you think she's truly ill.

Your basic point of reference is your daughter's behavior prior to the crisis. It's only natural that she be disheartened and glum for a while, perhaps for months. But if she is basically behaving in a way that was normal *for her* before the trauma, chances are she will be able to make a full recovery.

A week or so after a crisis, most people will begin to show signs of improvement. Maybe your daughter will take a walk or call a friend; her eating habits will begin to revert back to normal; she'll answer the phone messages that have been piling up. After about three weeks, if she's continued to improve, you can go ahead and start encouraging her to resume some of her former activities. All the while, you must keep reassuring her that you love her and are standing by with your arms outstretched should she need you to catch her again.

If your daughter does not appear to be recovering, schedule an appointment for her with a therapist or counseling center. You may also want to research the social-service agencies in your town that offer aid for people with emotional problems. No mother is equipped to handle her daughter's emotional disorders by herself, and it is extremely dangerous for you to try. Some depressed daughters really do give up, just as they've threatened to—they can't find meaning in their life or regain a sense of identity. Seriously depressed people really do kill themselves. If you fear your daughter might be one of these, get her the help she needs at once.

There are two other types of dependent daughters who require special attention beyond the scope of this book. They are the emotionally dependent daughter and the substance-dependent daughter, both of whom I'll briefly discuss at the end of this chapter. But the most common cases by far are those where the daughter has experienced a setback, relied on her parents for help, and then refused or been too frightened to stand on her own feet again. These daughters have redefined themselves as losers or victims. They believe they can't make it by themselves and that Mom has to rescue them.

What's in It for Mom?

"I'm her wailing wall, I'm her baby-sitter, I'm her bank, I'm her shoulder to cry on." Alberta, sixty-three, was filling me in on the background of her dependent daughter, Gail. The twenty-nine-year-old woman had been living with Alberta for nearly three years, having moved back into her childhood bedroom.

"Why have you let it go on for so long?" I asked. "Did it feel good at the beginning? Why does it bother you now?"

Alberta was silent for a moment, reflecting on the crisis that had pushed Gail back into her home. Then, slowly, she tried to reconstruct exactly how she had felt as Gail became more and more dependent on her.

> Gail was living with her boyfriend, a very nice young man whom we all thought would marry her. But it didn't work out. When he moved out of their apartment, she couldn't afford the rent by herself, so she moved back in with us.
>
> How did I feel about it? I felt terrible for her. He'd hurt her so badly, and I just wanted to make it all better. So I was happy to have her come back. In those first few months, Gail and I were closer than we'd been in a decade. She'd been quite an independent young woman, but this breakup really pulled the rug out from under her. She told me everything, and although I felt sorry for her, I remem-

ber thinking that one good part about this was that maybe she and I would get closer again. And to tell the truth, I was thrilled about that.

A feeling of greater intimacy with their daughters is a side benefit of dependency that most moms find hard to resist. The last time the two were really close was usually when the daughter was eleven or twelve and just entering puberty. As she starts to develop physically, a young girl will rely on her mother to educate her about such mysteries as bras, electric shavers, menstruation, and sex. These are formidable milestones that a girl typically regards with barely contained horror: "A bra? I don't want to wear a bra! I don't want to have boobs. I don't want to have a period. I don't want to have a baby." For a year or so, as the girl's body is changing, she and her mother form a very intimate bond.

Then adolescence arrives, and the teenage girl distances herself from her mother. This is normal and natural, but Mom misses their closeness desperately; she mourns for it. In most relationships, she and her daughter will never share that extreme intimacy again. So when a daughter returns ten or fifteen years later, her mom can't help but think, "We can pick up where we left off. We'll bake cookies together and go to the museum. Maybe the revival theater will show *Gone With the Wind* again."

It's all very, very seductive, and your daughter knows it. She realizes that there is a trade-off for your support, and the trade-off is emotional access to her. There is nothing innately manipulative about this, it's just a fact that if you ask for someone's help, that person is going to want to know why. The more details you give, the more likely it is that your rescuer will understand and sympathize with your predicament. If your rescuer is your mother, the details provide more than just enlightenment; they provide the intimacy she's been longing for. It's a huge bargaining chip on the daughter's part, and it takes a strong mother to see this dynamic for what it is early on in the crisis.

After about a year, Alberta realized that her daughter's confidences were somewhat halfhearted. Their intimacy began to feel like the forced, false negotiating tool that it actually was. Yet Alberta hung in there, determined to help Gail rebuild her life. Alberta, a no-nonsense, problem-solving type of woman, fell into the trap that ensnares so many rescuing moms. She began to act as if she were omnipotent, as if single-handedly she could fix all of her daughter's problems. What's more, she believed that it was her duty as a mother to keep on trying until she succeeded. She took over.

Mom, the All-powerful

There was one big flaw in Alberta's approach, although moms who are caught up in it rarely notice: the problem wasn't Alberta's, it was her daughter's. At issue wasn't whether Alberta could succeed at getting Gail back on track, but whether Gail could do it herself. The more money, dating tips, beauty advice, and career counseling Alberta gave her, the more Gail felt her mother was trying to control her. And many moms do relish the control they get as a result of their daughters' dependency.

"When I gave her money and listened to all her problems and most intimate secrets, I felt as if I were the expert," Alberta admitted. That can be an extremely gratifying feeling. It validates a mother's role as teacher—"See, I was right! You should have listened to me all along." It reaffirms her superior position. But when your daughter is an adult, you should view her as an equal, not a subordinate. It's wonderful if you're a good role model, because she'll always be looking to see how you handle your life. Maybe you'll inspire her. No matter how brilliantly you handle your life, however, you are not qualified to handle hers, too.

Think about it. Are you really such an expert? Are you a professional career counselor? Do you have the inside track on your local community colleges or the most recent information about student loans? Are you specially trained to research the best buys in cars or condos? Do you have a medical degree? What are you doing for her that she couldn't do for herself, or that someone with real knowledge in the field couldn't do better?

When you stop and consider it point by point, it's obvious that you do not know it all and cannot solve your daughter's problems for her. Not that you ever said to yourself, "I am omnipotent." It begins more subtly, for example, with a trip to the library to get her a few books about possible career paths. You feel strong and competent, while she appears weak and depressed, so why not help her out? It's a generous-enough impulse, but it doesn't usually end well. As you take over more and more details for her, she will only feel weaker and less able. As for the information itself, whether it's about careers, schooling, housing, or whatever, if she's not motivated enough to research it she's probably not motivated enough to actually attend a class or read a book. In fact, she's likely to reject your proposals precisely because they come from you. It's the only way she can exert her power; you're doing everything else.

Some daughters are so entrenched in their helplessness that they do require an extra push to make changes. In chapter six, I'll describe the most productive way to go about motivating such daughters. Without a specific plan and specific goals, however, doing your daughter's footwork for her can backfire by making her feel even more inadequate.

Guilt and Altruism

Not all rescuing mothers enjoy the control or crave the greater intimacy that comes with their daughter's dependency. Some are stuck in the rescuing role because of guilt. "She's my daughter," they explain. "I can't throw her out." Their view has been shaped by the myth that a mom must support her child, no matter what. Some of these mothers initially enjoy basking in the glow of their own altruism: "Look at all I'm doing for her. As a mother, I'm the cream of the crop. I will never say no to my daughter." These moms would do well to remember that most saints were also martyrs, and were only canonized years after their death. Eventually, your dependent daughter will demand so much from you that you'll feel more like a sucker than a saint.

While altruistic instincts may wear thin relatively quickly, guilt is much more difficult to deal with. Parents who are financially comfortable feel tremendous guilt about turning down their daughters' requests. "You can afford it," she may remind them, and it's true. Their friends, neighbors, and family all know they're well off, so what's their excuse for holding back? They themselves may be at a loss to explain their reluctance; shouldn't good parents help their children? Saying no to their daughter feels coldhearted, cheap, and wrong.

Once the guilt sets in, practicality goes out the window. Everything takes place on an emotional level, and it becomes nearly impossible to see the situation for what it really is: exploitative. All your daughter need do is remind you that you are *capable* of helping her, and you react as if you therefore *must* help her. She feels entitled to your aid, but she is not the only one involved in the decision. As purser, you have the right to decide how much you want to dole out. As her parent, you have the responsibility to decide how healthy it is for your daughter to live on the dole.

Helpless daughters can become expert at convincing you that life has dealt them a bad hand compared to you. It's certainly true that the cost of living is higher today than it was thirty years ago. "Gee, Mom," your daughter might say, "a one-bedroom apartment costs eight hundred dollars a month, and your mortgage is only three hundred and fifty dollars. Why don't I come stay with you for a while, pay you two hundred dollars a month rent, and we'll both save some money?" You feel sympathetic toward her so you agree, even though you don't need the money and prefer to live alone. Thus the entrapment begins. But remember, you are not all-powerful. You didn't create the current economic situation, and it is not up to you to even out the scales for your adult daughter. Ultimately, she must learn to play the hand life dealt her. If she doesn't, what will happen to her when you're not around to prop her up?

I'd never suggest that you deny yourself the pleasure of treating your daughter to a nice dinner once in a while, or a pretty sweater, or even a grand vacation if that's within your budget. But if she expects and demands it, it's no longer a gift and it no longer feels very pleasurable. In that case you must have the courage to end the exploitation, for her sake as well as yours. Yes, all parents should provide a safety net for their children in times of crisis, but keep in mind that a crisis has a beginning, a middle, and an end. It's not a continuing exhibition that you are required to fund.

No matter what strategy your daughter uses to convince you to keep opening your checkbook—playing on your pity, guilt-tripping you, threatening to cut you off—you must remember that the most valuable thing you can give her is not money. It is your belief in her ability to succeed on her own.

Why the Victim Resents the Rescuer

When your daughter first appealed to you for help, she probably made a pretty persuasive argument for herself. Most parents don't even need to be persuaded; they're happy to wire the money or clear out the spare bedroom. The daughter generally responds with sincere gratitude and, as I mentioned earlier, a new willingness to confide in her mom. High on the intimacy and her own sense of power, Mom will often relish these first weeks or months, even though she regrets that it was a crisis that brought her daughter back to her again.

As the situation starts to devolve into a full-blown "victim" and "rescuer" dynamic, however, Mom is in for a surprise. Princess Charming becomes a spoiled, complaining tyrant. *Gracious, helpful,* and *cooperative* are not words moms often use to describe their dependent daughters. *Sullen, angry,* and *hostile* are the adjectives of choice.

This is because the dependent "victim" always resents the person who is rescuing her. By rescuing your daughter, you are in essence saying, "I agree with you. You're not smart, talented, or competent enough to make it on your own. You can't do it without me, poor baby." Nothing could be worse for your daughter than this glaring vote of no confidence. She needs you to believe in her, no matter how helpless she is behaving. If you don't, it undermines her self-confidence worse than any setback in the outside world. Whether or not she is consciously aware of it, this is why she's so angry at you.

Dr. Stephen Karpman (1972) studied the dynamics of victims and rescuers and came up with a model I find very useful when trying to explain to moms why rescuing is a no-win situation. The model is called the Karpman Drama Triangle. One side represents the rescuer, the next side the victim, and the third, the persecutor. According to Karpman, the rescuer always ends up being a victim of the person she rescues. The original victim becomes a persecutor, complaining that the rescuer is not doing enough, or not doing it right, or not doing it with sufficient kindness.

I've definitely found this to be true with my clients and their helpless daughters. Mom can never do enough, and the more she tries—the longer the dependency drags on—the more demanding and ungrateful her daughter becomes. Inevitably, most mothers reach a breaking point, which is when they schedule an appointment with me. Sometimes Mom has been quietly losing her mind for many months and calmly makes a decision to stop the madness. More often, the daughter has done something so outrageous that it pushes past Mom's tolerance level. The two of them may be living in a one-bedroom apartment, and the daughter asks if her boyfriend can move in, too. Or the daughter announces she's pregnant. Or the bank calls to inform Mom that the daughter is forging her name on checks. Or the daughter puts her mother's house up for bail when she gets arrested. Then, Mom finally gets the message.

What About Dad?

If you are married, you and your husband have probably spent many a night in bed arguing about your helpless daughter (as she snoozed peacefully across the hall). Dad plays a pivotal role in the dependent-daughter dynamic because fathers are very susceptible to their daughters' pleas for help. A father's initial reaction to his daughter's crisis is usually to pull out the checkbook and then stand back, letting Mom take over the emotional part. Dad may be uncomfortable discussing his daughter's problems with her, but he still loves her dearly and wants to protect her. For that reason, your daughter may find an even more willing rescuer in your husband than in you.

When a victim wears out her original rescuer, she usually has a second one waiting in the wings. With a dependent daughter, that person is often Dad. Even if you and your husband began this episode in agreement ("We must help her!"), there might come a day when your paths split. That's when you decide your daughter is not so helpless, but your husband disagrees. Occasionally Dad sees the light first, but more often it's Mom who, after all those heart-to-hearts with her daughter, has a clearer sense of the young woman's emotional state and true potential.

The moment you start talking to your husband about reining in the support, your daughter will probably sense it and turn her attention to Dad. Then, with the intensity and canniness of a three-year-old, your grown daughter may attempt to play the two of you against each other. You must be prepared for this collusion and be committed to standing together, just as you did when she was a toddler learning the rules of the house. Otherwise your marriage is in for some rocky times.

It's likely that your daughter will have plenty of ammunition to work with if she does decide to divide and conquer. Bad vacations, missed opportunities, wrong choices, errant siblings—she knows every can of worms in the family cupboard. By opening a few, she might gain her father's allegiance or get you and him sniping at each other, thereby taking the focus off her. To guard against this, have your husband read this book, or at least chapters four, five, and six, before you begin to implement changes. That way the information will be coming from an objective observer (me) rather than a fed-up, angry mother (you). If your spouse is aware of the strategies used by his dependent daughter, he might be less vulnerable to her and more willing to work with you.

Second Dads

Stepfathers are in the unenviable position of having to watch their wife deal with a dependent daughter from the sidelines. In most cases, the second husband has little or no voice in the dependency drama being played out between his wife and stepdaughter. His opinions are rarely taken seriously; rather, Mom dismisses him with a remark such as "What do you know about my daughter and me? Stay out of this."

Mothers, be forewarned: there are grave consequences to ignoring your husband's input. The immediate result is that he'll feel impotent in his own house and unimportant in your eyes. This feeling of being left out can, and very often does, wreak havoc in a marriage. Many husbands give up hope of ever having a say about the dependent daughter and withdraw from the fray silently but with resentments brewing. Other men just walk. The dropout rate in second marriages is abysmal—much greater than in first marriages, especially if there are children from the previous unions.

In second marriages both partners bring so much history to the mix that they have little energy left over to deal with a problem child. First marriages have the bond of shared experiences, memories, and extended families to help them get through the crisis of a dependent daughter, but the roots are much shallower in a second marriage. In a first marriage your husband clearly has the right to express his opinion about his daughter, but no such entitlement exists in a second marriage; a mother must bestow it on her new spouse.

Mothers in this situation are caught between a rock and a hard place. They feel guilty for putting their daughter through a divorce (regardless of the reasons for the first marriage's breakup) and feel compelled to defend her behavior to their new mate. Since the behavior is often pretty indefensible, many moms deal with the conflict by shutting their husbands out. Before you do this, realize how hazardous it can be to your marriage. Be on the alert for ways your daughter might be manipulating the situation, and try to achieve some solidarity with your spouse and set up some ground rules for dealing with your daughter together. A therapist can give you suggestions and help you get perspective on the problem. Even one or two sessions can make a great difference.

The Sky Won't Fall If You Tell Her No

Underneath all the sympathy, psychological perks, and indecision, there is one fear shared by all parents of dependent daughters. They are all afraid they will lose their daughter's love if they say no to her. In its harshest sense, the dependent-daughter situation is little more than blackmail. Your daughter has something you want: her, or her and her children. You have something she wants: support. She has just one card to play, but it's so powerful that it keeps many parents enslaved for years.

Only by seeing a number of these cases, as I have, could you know that the fear of losing a daughter's love is usually unfounded. Most parents have never asked their daughter what she'll do if they refuse her, they just assume the worst. In fact, most daughters would be surprised to learn the depth of their parents' fears.

Colleen, fifty-eight, had been supporting her daughter Dana, twenty-four, at the family home for eighteen months before she finally worked up the courage to say no. It happened when Dana brought her boyfriend home and nonchalantly went into her bedroom with him, closing the door defiantly. "I saw red and went right in there after them," Colleen recounted. " 'Not in my house, you don't,' I told her.

> "It's my house, too," she sassed back.
>
> "Not anymore," I said. "I want you out of here by next Monday."
>
> As I walked down the hall I heard the boyfriend say, "I told you not to push it." And Dana said, "Yeah, well, I guess it's time to go." She left with him that afternoon— after a year and a half!—with no good-bye or word of thanks. I thought I wouldn't hear from her for months. No such luck. She was calling me up within the week, asking for money.

As we'll see in the next chapter, the dependent daughter is usually furious when her parents announce that the bank is closing. During the transition period, as she gets back on her feet, there are sure to be rough patches and nasty confrontations. Your daughter may openly refuse to see you or to let you see the grandkids—for a while. Or she may be more covert about it, suddenly becoming unavailable whenever you want to make plans with her. Realize, too, that by pushing your daughter out of the nest you probably *won't* be seeing as much of her as you used to; that's part of the deal. But it's the rare daughter who permanently ceases contact with her parents because they stop paying her bills. The cases where this does happen tend to involve extremely wealthy families.

The Emotionally Dependent Daughter

Most dependent daughters are addicted to their parents' check-book rather than their emotional support, but there are some whose dependency has nothing to do with money. Not only is emotional dependency frustrating for the mother, it also can become a crippling psychological handicap for her grown daughter. Over the years, the all-encompassing merger of Mom and Daughter takes on a life of its own.

In these instances Mom has become an alter ego for the daughter, confidently stepping in wherever the daughter fears to tread. This sort of dependency usually doesn't arise from a crisis, but evolves over many years. Often the daughter never really differentiates from her mom, never cuts the apron strings. As time goes by, her reliance on Mom becomes more pronounced: she can't buy a dress without Mom's approval, fly on an airplane without Mom, or give a party without Mom's help. She must phone Mom every morning and night, sometimes more often. She must spend every Sunday and holiday at Mom's house, and frequently stops in a few nights a week as well.

In the beginning—for instance, when the daughter is just out of college—Mom may revel in this closeness. It might make her feel needed and powerful to provide all the answers for her daughter. But this level of psychological dependency in a grown woman, even one who is just in her early twenties, is not healthy. If your daughter fits this description, you must begin to wean her away from you. You may have to sacrifice some of the intimacy you now share with her, but that intimacy is actually dependency, and your daughter is paying for it with her emotional well-being.

Start out slowly. Decision by decision, step back. If she needs your help buying a dress, tell her to choose three first, and then weigh in with your opinion. Gently let her know that she doesn't need to call you every day; once or twice a week will be fine.

Reassure her that you love her and are interested in her life, and use "I" statements when you're declining to help her, so it takes the emphasis off her neediness: "I can't meet you at the mall today; I've got some bills to pay. I'm sure I'll like the dress you choose." Or "It makes me a little uncomfortable always having to be home for your evening phone call. I'd feel better knowing that we'll have a nice long chat on the weekend."

If your daughter seems extremely anguished about these changes, I strongly urge the two of you to set up a meeting with a counselor. There's a good chance it's your daughter who really needs the help, but you may have more luck getting her into the therapist's office if you go with her for the first few sessions. Emotionally dependent daughters often need the extra support of a therapist as they learn to ride through life without Mom's hand on the back of the bicycle seat.

How Can I Help Get Her Sober?

The advice in this book is useless if your daughter is addicted to drugs or alcohol. I'm aware that many substance abusers are dependent on their parents, and my heart goes out to everyone in these families, but over the years I've developed a somewhat inflexible philosophy about substance abusers. It comes down to this. If your dependent daughter is abusing drugs or alcohol, your first obligation is to yourself, not her. Save your own life before small parts start to die off with every emergency her problem creates.

After many grim hours of client counseling, I've become a staunch advocate of the tough-love school. Until your daughter is ready to go into a rehab program (they are available in every city), you should not give her money or shelter. If you do you will be enabling her, that is, helping her to stay addicted. You must understand that as much as you love her, you cannot cure her. The mother of an addicted daughter often gets caught in the addict's web, but luckily there are programs for family members, too: Families Anonymous, Because I Love You, Tough Love, and many others address both the addict and her family.

When you're dealing with an addict, the only help you should offer is support in her recovery efforts. You can drive her to the rehab center or twelve-step meetings; you can visit her in rehab; you can pay for the programs (with a check made out to the program, not to her). Any other type of help is just more enabling.

"What'll happen to her?" is the frantic response I often get to my "hard-line" approach. There's a possibility your daughter will hit bottom. You have to let her do this, whether it means being arrested, landing in a homeless shelter, or wallowing in the gutter. That's what it sometimes takes to make an addict admit she has a problem. If you bail her out every time and then try to reason with her, you're fooling yourself. You are not talking to your daughter, you're talking to the drug. It's a very tough decision, but you have to let her go. You may even lose her for a while—but she's already lost to you. Admit you are helpless in order to help her.

As heartbreaking as it is to have an addicted daughter, there are many success stories. Get in a program, remember always that you are not omnipotent and cannot solve this problem for her, and offer your emotional support when your daughter agrees to get help. That's as much as you can or should do for her.

Independence Day

Your dependent daughter will not be happy when you tell her you're taking away the crutches. You'll need to be prepared for tirades, guilt trips, slammed doors, and pleading phone calls. But no matter how frightened or hostile she may be at first, in the end—when she is supporting herself and has regained her dignity—your daughter will understand your decision. She may not thank you for it, at least not out loud, but in her soul she'll know that you believed in her. In the next chapter, I'll show you the steps that will lead to the independence both you and she deserve.

Writing the Independence Contract

*It's not that I can't afford to help her. I can, and she knows it—
that's part of the problem! My daughter works part-time as a
radio announcer, but she has the unshakable conviction that I
should pay off her student loans, pay half her rent, and basically
provide her with the finer things in life. When I object, she yells at
me and tells me I'm selfish and manipulative. How do I get out of
this?*

—*R u t h ,   a g e   f i f t y - s e v e n*

$\mathcal{D}$EPENDENT DAUGHTERS AND THEIR MOTHERS ARE IN-
volved in a complex emotional drama that can go on for years
before Mom reaches her breaking point. But inevitably the day
does arrive when, desperate, furious, or nearly broke, Mom vows
to stop supporting her daughter. The question is, how?

The single most effective tool I've developed for weaning a
dependent daughter is called the independence contract. This
document, which both mother and daughter sign, spells out the
terms of Mom's declining support over a specific period of time.
After that period (usually six to nine months), support will cease
altogether or be reduced to a level with which Mom is comfort-

able. Even if your relationship with your daughter seems impossibly knotted up, this contract will enable you to regain control of your life, time, and money.

Prep Work: Thinking It All Through

Before you draw up the contract and confront your daughter, you must consider every aspect of your current circumstances. By carefully preparing yourself, you'll be able to follow through on your decisions and stand up to your daughter's resistance. And make no mistake—she will resist!

Your first move is to gauge whether your daughter actually is too ill to fend for herself. The guidelines in chapter four should help you there. If you have doubts about her mental state, you'll need to find a psychiatrist who can give you a clear assessment of her capabilities. Remember, there are many government-funded programs for adults who are mentally challenged. Even people with autism, Down's syndrome, and other serious conditions often live away from their family and hold down some sort of job. You need not personally bear the entire responsibility for your dependent daughter.

Most dependent daughters are not mentally ill. If yours seems capable of handling herself in everyday society, you may proceed to the next step. Write down every penny of support you provide for her. You need to know precisely what she's getting in order to construct a fair independence contract. The worksheet on pages 89–90 lists the most common goods and services parents supply, but it's not all-inclusive; your situation could be different.

If your daughter is living with you, you might not be able to attach a dollar amount to food, housing, utilities, and so forth, but you can approximate it by comparing your expenses before and after she moved in. It's not essential that you know these numbers, because what's really relevant is how much she'll need to live on her own, and that's not necessarily going to be equal to what she's costing you. (For example, her rent might cost more than a portion of your mortgage.) However, some parents are interested in seeing these figures either to satisfy their curiosity or prove to their daughter that her existence in their home does affect their cash flow.

If your daughter is living on her own but you are paying her bills, it's crucial that you and she are aware of the total amount of money you are supplying so that you can slowly turn off the faucet without leaving her high and dry too quickly.

Monthly Level of Support

Rent or mortgage   _____

Food   _____

Clothing   _____

Utilities   _____

Phone bill   _____

Day care   _____

Car payments   _____

Car insurance   _____

Medical care or insurance   _____

Medications   _____

Dental care or insurance   _____

Tuition   _____

Therapy   _____

Credit cards   _____

Miscellaneous debts   _____

Spending money   _____

Make sure you show this worksheet to your husband and find out how much money he is supplying to your daughter unbeknownst to you. Dads are notorious for slipping their daughters a twenty-dollar bill here, a fifty there. Ask him to tell you if he's been paying off any loans or credit cards. Now is the time to come clean, since it's vital that you and he are united in your plans.

You now have a snapshot of your daughter's level of dependency. Hurts, doesn't it? If you feel the fury rising, go sit in your car, shut the windows, and scream for a few minutes. Do not race into the living room and hurl the list in your daughter's lap. We're working out a strategy here; you'll confront her when you're calm and prepared.

How Much Support Should You Keep Giving Her?

The money you're giving your daughter falls into two categories: living expenses and debts. You need to determine which, if any, of these bills you are willing to keep paying after the independence contract is over. It's not necessary that you pay for anything at all. Many parents, however, are willing to keep providing certain goods or services; they just want to set boundaries.

Living expenses are items such as rent, utilities, and spending money. They will be with your daughter always, so be very careful which of these you agree to keep on funding. In my view your daughter is better off paying for these basics without your help. If she's always relying on a check from you, she'll never know the security of being able to support herself. She must get used to a standard of living that she can maintain on her own.

Debts, such as car payments and medical bills, might be costly but at some point they'll be paid off. If you feel inclined to continue offering your daughter some support, I recommend paying for debts rather than living expenses. At least there's a light at the end of the tunnel.

Tuition is in a class by itself; depending on your daughter's plans, it could be a short-term expenditure or one that extends for years into the future. The same goes for day care and tuition for your grandchildren. If you commit to long-term expenses such as these, your daughter should allow you to take an active role in deciding which facilities the kids will be attending.

Your daughter's therapy is a special case, too. If you feel that the therapist is helping her become more self-reliant and stable, you might want to continue paying for the sessions (directly to the therapist) after the six- or nine-month contract is up. Needless to say, if you disapprove of the therapist's approach or the effect he or she is having on your daughter, you'd be foolish to pay for the sessions. (See chapter six for more about dealing with your daughter's therapist.)

The following three questions will help you determine which items to keep funding.

1. *Do you want to keep paying for it?* If you want to provide certain non-living-expense items, such as dance lessons for your granddaughter, by all means do so. If you have doubts that the money will get into the proper hands, make payments directly to the dance studio, not to your daughter.

2. *Can you afford it?* This question is tricky, since many moms will hem and haw and say, "Well, yes, technically I can afford it," when in fact they are doing without basics in order to pay for their daughter's extras. Don't. You deserve your money as much as your daughter does, if not more.

3. *Did you promise to pay for it?* If you promised to pay for a specific item, such as school tuition, dental work, or a car, follow through *if you can afford to.* Just don't become a victim of your own shortsighted promises. If you made a commitment under duress or against your better judgment, you can change your mind. No one will come and arrest you.

There is a strong possibility that your daughter won't be terribly grateful for the items you continue to fund. She's going to focus on what she's losing, not what she's keeping. If you're paying for something because you hope it will assuage her anger, you'll probably be disappointed. Base your gift giving on what feels fair and comfortable to you, not on what you think your daughter's reaction might be.

Once you've made your decisions, stick to them, at least for the initial six- or nine-month period. Your daughter is going to perceive the independence contract as a tremendous shift in the rules you've both been playing by, which it is. The new rules are necessary, but you must stay committed to them. If you don't, your daughter will get the impression that the contract is flimsy.

The items you decide to keep paying for can be useful negotiating tools, particularly if there are grandchildren involved. But if you feel in your heart that it's best to withdraw all funding, follow your instincts. The bottom line is that you can't buy your daughter's love anyway. By writing the independence contract, you are telling her, "I love you enough to say no to you. I believe in you enough to help you change, even if it means you'll go through some scary times. Maybe you need to feel scared and deprived in order to get motivated. I trust that you'll still love me even when I'm not paying your bills."

The Grandma Day Care Center Is Closing

Withdrawing your baby-sitting services is different from withdrawing your financial support, because the grandchildren's welfare is directly affected. Many grandmas play surrogate mommy to their grandchildren because they believe they're better at mothering than their daughters. That may be true, but the fact remains that your daughter is still their mother. You already brought up your family; you aren't required to bring up hers as well.

If your daughter is an uninterested, mediocre mom, there are parenting courses she can take or family therapy sessions she can attend to improve herself. She must go through a maturation process and accept her rightful role as her children's mother. If you're always taking up the slack for her, why should she bother? As long as she is not physically or verbally abusing her kids, it's time she learns to be a good parent. (Abusive mothers need intensive therapy, and sometimes their children do need to be removed from the home. As I stated back in chapter one, this book is not intended for abusive moms.)

Sometimes a dependent daughter will claim she can't work unless Grandma watches the kids. Unless you genuinely desire to sign on for this tremendously taxing job, you'll probably need to research the day care facilities in your area so you can present your daughter with an alternative. There are many excellent day care programs and preschools in a wide range of prices. Churches and synagogues have preschools, and government programs may also be available. Check out all the options before you write your contract, and include a day care plan in it. Naturally you'll continue to be a loving, supportive figure in the lives of your grandchildren, but unless they are very young or in danger at their mother's hands, base your baby-sitting schedule on what's reasonable for you, not what's convenient for your daughter.

Some grandmothers do choose to continue caring for their grandchildren full-time every day. After the youngsters are three years old, however, it's a good idea to enroll them in preschool at least part-time so they get exposure to other children and to the toys and learning tools the schools have to offer. It's rather unusual for a grandma to want full responsibility for her young grandchildren—most of us are too tired for it! Ask yourself why you're willing to do this. Some grandmothers provide unlimited baby-sitting in order to control their daughter and her family or to be assured a role in her life. These reasons don't have the child's best interest at heart.

Some people believe that when it comes to looking after a child, any family member is preferable to a day care center or preschool. I'm not about to jump into the middle of that debate, but will only urge you to consider your situation honestly. Is your grandchild interacting with other children, getting plenty of opportunities to play and exercise, and developing at a rate comparable to other kids the same age? Or do you and the child spend many hours at home alone, in front of the television? Can you keep up with your grandchild's energy level, or are you continually asking him or her to slow down and be quiet? If you feel you might be hindering the youngster's growth but are uneasy about bowing out entirely, perhaps you could suggest a compromise to your daughter. For instance, you could care for the child in the afternoon, so your daughter doesn't have to rush home from work and your grandchild won't be spending too many hours in day care.

Think carefully about the dynamic between you, your daughter, and your grandchildren, and try to do what's right for the young ones and healthy for you and your daughter. If you have a hard time figuring it out on your own, schedule a session or two with a family therapist before you write your independence contract. The therapist can help you sift through your emotions, fears, and motives so that you can come to a wise decision.

Writing the Independence Contract

The independence contract is designed to do two things: motivate your daughter to be responsible for herself, and get you and her relating to each other on a more honest level. By writing down the terms of your relationship, you bring it all out into the open. It is absolutely necessary to write the contract, sign it, and see that she signs it, too. Just talking about the issues won't accomplish anything; it won't seem real to your daughter.

Your mission is to withdraw financial aid to your daughter at a rate that gives her time to reestablish herself. The amounts you pay should be based on what you can afford now, not on what you have been paying in the past.

The following are two boilerplate independence contracts, one for daughters who are living with their moms and the other for daughters who are living on their own but are financially dependent on Mom. Fill in the blanks based on the worksheet on pages 89–90. If you can't afford to offer the level of support outlined in the contract below, tailor it to your own circumstances. Keep in mind that there are many types of housing arrangements; if paying for an apartment is out of your price range, your daughter can always rent a room in a house.

Independence Contract for Live-in Daughters

I, your mother, hereby agree to do the following:

I will pay first and last month's rent on an apartment, if the rent does not exceed $ _____ .

I will pay your rent for the first three months, after which I will pay half of your rent for the next three months. I expect you to have a job by that time.

Until six months are up, I will give you $ _____ each month to pay for

_____

_____

_____

After six months, I will give you $ _____ each month for three more months to pay for

_____

At the end of nine months you will be on your own. It took nine months for your gestation, and I figure it will take nine months for your differentiation.

(Optional—for those of you who want to provide ongoing support for specific items such as car payments, tuition, etc.) In addition to the above, I will continue to pay for _____ until _____ .

(Optional—for those of you who wish to curtail baby-sitting duties). I will continue to look after (*children's names*) for one month. After that time, you will enroll (*names*) in a day care center or preschool. If you have not selected a school by that time, I have already signed (*names*) up for (*day care center or school's name*). I will pay for the day care for three months. After that time, I will pay for half of the day care for another three months. At the end of six months, you will be fully responsible for the day care fees.

I will be available at all times to support you emotionally and encourage your development. I will not be available for your financial needs.

Please note that this agreement in no way is to interfere with my visiting my grandchildren. My relationship with them is separate from my financial differentiation from you. I hope we can amicably work out these arrangements so we will all have our needs met.

Daughter, I love you enough to set you free.

_____   _____
Date   (Mom's name)

Daughter's Agreement

I agree to the terms set down by my mother. I will not prevent my mother from visiting with my children. If I run into problems during this transitional period, I will attempt to solve them on my own without asking my mother for money. I look forward to a new relationship with my mother, in which we will both effect change.

_____   _____
Date   (Daughter's name)

Independence Contract for Financially Dependent Daughters

I, your mother, hereby agree to do the following:

I will continue to pay your rent for the next three months, (*name the months*). After that, I will pay half of your rent for the following three months. I expect you to have a job by that time or to have moved into housing that you can afford on your own, without assistance from me.

Until six months are up, I will give you $ _____ each month to pay for

_____

_____

_____

After six months, I will give you $ _____ each month for three more months to pay for

_____

At the end of nine months you will be on your own. It took nine months for your gestation, and I figure it will take nine months for your differentiation.

(*Optional—for those of you who want to provide ongoing support for specific items such as car payments, tuition, etc.*) In addition to the above, I will continue to pay for

_____

until _____ .

(*Optional—for those of you who wish to curtail baby-sitting duties*). I will continue to look after (*children's names*) for one month. After that time, you will enroll (*names*) in a day care center or preschool. If you have not selected a school by that time, I have already signed (*names*) up for (*day care center or school's name*). I will pay for the day care for three months. After that, I will pay for half of the day care for another three months. At the end of six months, you will be fully responsible for the day care fees.

I will be available at all times to support you emotionally and encourage your development. I will not be available for your financial needs.

Please note that this agreement in no way is to interfere with my visiting my grandchildren. My relationship with them is separate from my financial differentiation from you. I hope we can amicably work out these arrangements so we will all have our needs met.

Daughter, I love you enough to set you free.

_____   _____
Date   (Mom's name)

Daughter's Agreement

I agree to the terms set down by my mother. I will not prevent my mother from visiting with my children. If I run into problems during this transitional period, I will attempt to solve them on my own without asking my mother for money. I look forward to a new relationship with my mother, in which we will both effect change.

_____   _____
Date   (Daughter's name)

Countdown to D day

Write the independence contract in longhand on a sheet of paper, print it out on your computer, or photocopy it from this book and fill in the blanks. Make two copies, one for you and one for your daughter.

If you're married, go over the final contract with your husband, asking him again for his support and commitment. Remind him that the one who benefits the most from these changes is your daughter. As her parents, you must encourage her to reach her potential and take responsibility for herself. It's ideal if he has read chapters four, five, and six of this book, but some men will put off the reading indefinitely. You don't want to lose momentum waiting for him, so carry on as best you can and explain the principles to him yourself.

What about your other children—should you tell them your plans or ask for their support? Absolutely not. It's crucial that you keep this contract strictly between your daughter and you (and your husband). Telling your other children will make your dependent daughter feel ganged up on, and that will only add to her anxiety. When you break the news to her, be sure to tell her that the contract is confidential. If she wants to show her siblings, it's up to her. Reassure her that whether or not she tells her brothers and sisters, you will not be discussing her situation with them.

Your other children may applaud or criticize your actions, but either way it's none of their business. If they approach you about their sister, just tell them that you promised her you wouldn't discuss your arrangement. It's always a mistake to gossip to one child about another, but in the case of a dependent daughter, it's particularly risky.

Let's Talk

Now, with independence contract in hand and your plans crystal clear in your own mind, you're ready for the big confrontation. As I've mentioned before, it may not be pleasant, so I advise meeting with your daughter in a public place where she'll be more likely to behave herself. A restaurant is the logical choice. A public setting is more equitable for your daughter, too, because it's neutral territory. Breaking the news at your kitchen table, where you feel powerful enough to plan the invasion of Normandy, really isn't fair to her.

Set up the date in advance, at a specific time. As you drive to the restaurant, try to keep the conversation light and pleasant. If your daughter senses your nervousness, brush it off with a casual remark such as "I've got a bit of a headache." The point is, you don't want to begin your discussion until you are seated and have placed your order. If you start talking seriously en route, you may never get out of the car, and your calm conversation might deteriorate into a shouting match.

Keep the independence contract in your purse as you settle in for your meal—you're not going to show it to your daughter until you've shared a few serious reflections. You'll begin with, "Let's talk. I need to tell to you about some of the changes I'm going to be making in my life. I'm different than the way you know me to be. I've changed."

Speak about *your* feelings, *your* decisions. Use "I" messages, not "you" messages. At all costs, do not accuse your daughter, as in: "You're bleeding me dry!" If you accuse her she'll immediately start defending herself, and that is not the way you want the conversation to go.

The conversation should proceed like this:

1. Explain how you felt when your daughter first asked for your help. This should include the reassurance that you love her a lot, which is why you were happy to help her.

2. Explain how you feel now—angry, exploited, hurt, frustrated, whatever. Tell her that things are not working out as they now stand and that you have decided to curtail your financial support of her.

3. Hand her the independence contract and let her read it.

4. Duck!

Explain how you felt at the beginning. You might begin by reminding your daughter of the original crisis and the duration of her dependency: "Two years ago, when you lost your job, I felt very badly for you and wanted to do everything I could to help you." Include your husband whenever you can, to stress that the two of you are in sync on this: "Your father and I will always be there for you in a crisis."

You should also confess the not-so-noble aspects of your rescue mission, which you learned about in chapter four. You might admit that you saw her bad break as an opportunity to get closer to her, or that you secretly enjoyed the control her dependency gave you. Whatever the truth is about your motives, tell her. That gets the conversation off to an honest start and keeps her from feeling defensive. And be sure to tell her that you love her.

Explain how you feel now. By confessing your ignoble motives, you can segue nicely into the next phase of the conversation. You'll say, "Now I realize that I've made a big mistake. I've undermined you, and I shouldn't have done that. What's happened is, even though I agreed to support you, I've begun to feel very exploited."

As you say these words, you might feel your blood begin to boil. The minute this happens, tell her. If you talk about your anger, you'll keep yourself from lashing out at your daughter. "I'm angry because I feel you've taken advantage of me. I accept my part in that, but I need things to be different now."

With this statement, your daughter will probably hear the alarming sound of the money train pulling out of the station.

"What do you mean? How different?" she'll demand. And so, you'll drop the bomb: "I'm no longer willing to support you to the extent that I have been. I'm not going to cut you off all at once, but I've written down a plan for us. It'll let you be more self-sufficient, and it will help us build a new relationship." Again, if you are married, mention your husband's involvement: "Daddy and I are no longer willing . . . We've written down a plan. . . ."

Hand her the independence contract. Take the contract out of your purse and hand it to your daughter. Don't defend yourself, don't explain it; just let her read the whole thing. Sit silently and let it sink in.

Duck! Unfortunately, many daughters see red when they read the contract and instantly begin to threaten or verbally abuse their mom: "If you do this, you'll never see me again!" your daughter might say. Or she may simply let flow a string of expletives, then turn and stomp out of the restaurant after tossing the (unsigned) contract down on the table. If she's more fearful than hostile, she may break down and cry, or even threaten suicide. Be as compassionate as you can, but be firm.

Whatever emotional flotsam she heaves at you, imagine that you are putting it into a shoe box and placing it on the highest shelf in your closet. Don't dwell on it, and don't let her shake your resolve. Your daughter doesn't really mean it; she's just in a state of shock. Trust me, there are very few daughters who never talk to their mothers again after showdowns such as this.

Getting Past Her Resistance

As your daughter storms out of the restaurant in tears, you might be flooded with guilt and regret. Take a deep breath, and rest assured that you've done the right thing. Remember, you thought this through over a period of days or weeks; you've come to your decision rationally. Don't let the emotion of the moment undercut your plans.

Your next move is clear. Simply wait until your daughter asks you for something—cash, the car keys, rent money—and when she does, say, "I'm not going to give you anything until we meet again and agree on this contract." She may very well hang up on you (or retreat to her room, slamming the door). Not to worry. She'll eventually come around; they always do. You must stand your ground. Some daughters, instead of giving the cold shoulder, resort to pleading. Do not cave in! Give her nothing until she finishes the discussion and signs the contract.

Don't allow more than one week to pass before attempting to open the lines of communication again. If you haven't heard from your daughter by then, call her and say, "Let's get together and discuss this. I'm going to tell you what I'm willing to do, and what I'm not willing to do." If she refuses to meet, just continue to withhold the money. You'd be surprised what a motivator this is. Keep calling, week by week. As her funds run out, she'll become more willing to talk. Sooner or later, you'll sit down again with your daughter and finish your discussion. If you're lucky, you may even finish it at the restaurant where it began—not every daughter goes off in a huff.

Once the discussion resumes, get ready to defend your position. Most daughters will feel genuinely betrayed by your new approach. "But I only asked you for a thousand a month," she might argue, "and you agreed and now you won't do it any more." I mentioned earlier that it's a good idea to honor specific promises if you are financially able. Open-ended cash handouts do not fall into this category. This isn't a court of law with a judge who will hand down some wise decision about what you "promised" your daughter. It's your life, your money. Simply tell your daughter that you made an error in judgment and you are now going to do things differently.

If your daughter seems frightened and panicky, reassure her that you'll always be there if another crisis erupts: "I'm not abandoning you; I'm releasing you from bondage to me. I believe with all my heart that you're up to the challenge, and I'll always be here to help you make this work."

After your daughter realizes that you're committed to the contract, fear or stubborn refusal may be her next response. "I can't do it," she may declare. "I'm just not ready." Depending on the relationship you have with her, you might consider asking some pointed questions about her state of mind. In some instances, mom and daughter have never spoken honestly about the daughter's neediness. Maybe your daughter has some concerns you never imagined.

I've listed some questions clients of mine have used in these talks with their daughters. You needn't phrase them as exactly as I've written them here; say them in a way that's natural for you.

Daughter, What's Going On?

- What makes you so certain that you can't fend for yourself?
- Do you prefer being helpless to being competent?
- Do you know the difference between being taken care of and being cared for?
- When I pity you, do you feel loved?
- Don't you resent me for having so much power over you?
- I feel that money has become a substitute for love with us. What do you think?
- Do you ask for my advice to keep me tethered to you?
- How long did you expect me to keep supporting you?
- Do you feel it's my duty to support you?
- Do you see me as a person, or just as a parent?

You probably won't reach a lightening-bolt revelation during this discussion, but that's not your goal. You are simply trying to steer the relationship onto a more honest course. Admitting (again) your past motives in the dependency cycle might make your daughter feel safe enough to risk a little soul-searching of her own. The greater her understanding of her dependency, the more open she may be to change. Whatever you do, don't sabotage the conversation by trying to pry an apology out of her or prodding her to admit she's been wrong.

If after a few gentle questions your daughter becomes hostile or unwilling to talk, let it go. As long as she signs the independence contract, you've completed your mission. If the discussion breaks down and she walks out on you again, keep calm and stand firm. Proceed as before, with weekly reminders, and have faith that eventually she'll come around.

Finally, perhaps weeks after your first confrontation, your daughter will sign the independence contract. Psychologically, this is a huge step for her—she has, in theory, agreed to your proposal. In chapter six I'll show you how to make certain she follows through.

Keeping Her Motivated

I've been paying for my grandson's day care so my daughter could go to school, but today I found out she stopped going to classes two months ago. She's just been sitting at home. I'm livid! We had agreed she'd finish the Licensed Practical Nurse program; then she'd be able to provide for her son. She uses my concern for him to manipulate me. How can I get her to honor her commitments and become responsible? Does my grandson have to suffer just so I can prove a point to my daughter?

—Dorothy, age fifty-nine

SIGNING THE INDEPENDENCE CONTRACT IS A SIGNIFICANT milestone, and I wish I could say that once your daughter takes this step your problems are over. In truth, things can get bumpy. Your daughter may try to undermine the plan, consciously or unconsciously. Emergencies may arise, either real or trumped-up, that threaten to stall the process indefinitely. Or you and your husband may lose your nerve and sabotage the contract yourselves. In this chapter I'll alert you to the most common stumbling blocks parents face when implementing the independence contract, and I'll explain the most effective ways to overcome them.

Fear is at the core of your daughter's resistance to change. Laziness may be a part of it, but beneath the laziness is dread. What if she really isn't smart enough to make it on her own? What if she tries and fails? Will you still be there for her? Although they might seem far-fetched to you, her fears are probably genuine. It's unsettling to see your once-confident daughter shrink back and claim that she's too scared to go on a job interview. On the one hand, your heart goes out to her. On the other, you're skeptical—can she possibly be that fragile, or is she manipulating you again? Since you'll never know the truth, take her fears at face value and deal with them sensibly and compassionately.

Your resounding theme throughout the weaning process should be that you are freeing your daughter, not marooning her: "I'm not leaving town. I'm not ignoring you. I'm helping you to become the person you were meant to be. You may feel I'm being cruel to you, but I'm not going to be around forever. It's time for you to take care of yourself—I know you can do it."

"But I'm afraid," she may insist.

"I know you are," you'll respond. "I'm afraid for you, too. I'm afraid of what's going to happen to you if you don't learn to be self-sufficient. What we're going to do is confront those fears. The more frightened you are, the quicker you'll want to get to a safe place. There's a lot of nervous energy in fear—let's harness that energy and get going on our plans."

The independence contract spells out all the aspects of self-reliance your daughter is striving for. But each step along the way, she may find reasons to object. "My therapist says I'm not ready . . . I don't have a car . . . the right clothes . . . the confidence . . . a resumé. . . ." And in each instance you'll reply, "That's all right. We're going to achieve the goals of this contract by tackling them one problem at a time."

"My Therapist Says I'm Not Ready"

Is your daughter's therapist friend or foe? My clients express a wide range of attitudes on the subject, from gratitude (Thank goodness my daughter has someone else to complain to!) to suspicion (I don't understand all that jargon he's telling her), to outright resentment (Why does she need a therapist? Why can't she come to me?). A great many dependent daughters are or have been in therapy, so it's no surprise if, after Mom hands them the independence contract, they appeal to the therapist for a "professional" sanction of their helplessness. Most good therapists are not so easily manipulated; most encourage their clients' moves toward autonomy and self-reliance. But there are some unfortunate exceptions.

Helen, fifty-seven, had been seeing me for about six months before she worked up the courage to write an independence contract for her daughter Annie, thirty-two. As she had feared, Annie responded by taking the issue to her therapist.

> Annie keeps telling me she's not ready to move out of my house, and she says her therapist backs her up. Well then, why doesn't the therapist feed her, pay her medical bills, and make her car payments? I'm getting very angry and resentful, mostly at the therapist, who seems to be controlling both my daughter and me.

Moms commonly make two mistakes when it comes to therapists. First, they overestimate the therapist's abilities. You should never assume that the therapist knows more about your daughter than you do; after all, you raised her. And there are factors to consider besides professional credentials. Maybe your daughter is manipulating or lying to the therapist. Or maybe the therapist is not experienced in mother-daughter relationships. Until you discuss the situation with the therapist yourself, you have no way of gauging his or her skills. Which leads us to mistake number two: Moms tend to accept their daughter's version of the therapy session without question.

"My therapist says I'm just not ready for such a big change," your daughter may announce. "She says I need at least six more months." Rather than backing down, you must respond to these reports by offering to talk to the therapist personally—either with or without your daughter. "Let's get together with your therapist and work out a plan. Have her call me, or set up a meeting for the three of us." If your daughter refuses to let you talk to her therapist, that's her right. But by the same token, you don't have to follow the therapist's advice when it's nothing more than hearsay from your daughter. Firmly tell her that if she won't let you talk with the therapist, the independence contract stands as you've written it.

It's not inconceivable that your daughter is twisting her therapist's words to suit her own purposes. Given that possibility, you may want to ponder the therapy issue in a new light. If the therapist seems to have had a positive effect on your daughter in the past, he or she might be an ally in the weaning process. Moms often worry that the therapist will automatically be on the daughter's side, but we therapists are well aware that there are two sides to every conflict. Having a therapist mediate a few sessions between you and your daughter can fuel-inject the independence program. If all three of you can work out an understanding, it provides your daughter with that much more impetus to get moving.

Since your daughter is the therapist's client, you will not be able to set up a meeting unless she agrees to it. The therapist will not go against your daughter's wishes and force her or trick her into a meeting. If your daughter is willing to cooperate, you'll have to meet her halfway. You'll need to be honest about your role in her dependency and willing to listen to her point of view. During the course of your sessions together, the therapist might ask you to fine-tune the contract. The prudent mom will be open to suggestions. In most cases, having the therapist's support of the process is well worth a few compromises.

There's always the possibility that when the three of you meet your daughter's therapist will vehemently oppose the contract. If that happens and you believe the therapist is off base, seek a second opinion. Schedule a session with another therapist and, if you feel comfortable with that person, ask him or her to meet with you, your daughter, and her therapist. Or have the two therapists collaborate on the case. "Dueling" therapists may seem a little extreme, but sometimes you have to fight fire with fire. One mom told me that she'd get phone calls from the therapist demanding cash on behalf of her daughter: "Theresa needs more money. You have to send her a check." This sort of request is unethical and entirely out of bounds, but a mom might not know exactly how to handle it. If your daughter and her therapist seem to be ganging up on you, bring in your own expert. Happily, things don't often disintegrate to that point.

The optimal situation is that you, your daughter, and her therapist get together and agree on a plan. In many cases the daughter refuses to do this, and the mom simply sticks to the original terms of the contract. Once the daughter realizes that her mother won't be moved by hearsay, those three grating words—"My therapist says . . ."—gradually fade from her repertoire.

"I'm Afraid to Live Alone"

Feeling safe in Mother's home is usually an illusion. What is a sixty-year-old mom going to do to protect her thirty-five-year-old daughter if, say, a burglar breaks in? But pointing this out to your daughter is probably useless—it's the childhood feeling of protection she's clinging to, not the present-day reality. She won't feel comfortable with the idea of living on her own until she's settled into her new home, the sooner the better.

My clients relate all sorts of fears to me from the mouths of their dependent daughters. Some sound as if they should be coming from an octogenarian, not a thirty-something: "What if I get sick and nobody knows it? What if I can't get to a phone? What if I fall down in the middle of the night?" Not every fear is unreasonable or neurotic—women who've been the victim of a crime may understandably suffer a lifelong terror of living alone.

Don't minimize your daughter's fears. Acknowledge them sympathetically, but stand your ground: "I know you're uncomfortable living alone, but honey, that's something you'll have to work out. You can rent an apartment in a high-security building or live with roommates. Let's go to the apartment rental agency tomorrow morning and look at the options." Your internal mantra must always be, "I am not omnipotent. I can't solve her every problem and make the world safe for her. Her only hope is to learn to live on her own."

"I'm Afraid to Go On a Job Interview"

"I am living with a terrified daughter," Jolie, fifty-one, told me.

> Samantha has always worked, but it was for family or friends. Now she's exhausted all those resources. She never had to go on a job interview, and she's so fearful she's begun to sleep away her days to avoid dealing with this. Her unemployment insurance is running out this month, and I can't even get her to read the want ads. Aside from planting a bomb under her bed, how do I get her motivated?

Jolie's daughter was twenty-six when she first had to face that most gut-wrenching of ordeals, the job interview. Most people have already endured a few interviews by that age, but looking for work is never easy or fun. When a daughter is dependent because she's lost her job, the interview can take on monstrous proportions. The longer she's out of the loop, the less confident she feels about her looks, poise, work history, and ability to do the job.

Once a daughter's confidence has bottomed out this badly, there is no way a mom can single-handedly bolster it up again. Naturally you want to cheer her on, but your daughter needs contact with people *other than Mom* to build her self-esteem to the point where she can take on that first interview. Every city has free or inexpensive programs that teach adults how to dress for a job interview, fill out applications, prepare a resumé, and so forth. The counselors will walk your daughter through practice interviews until she feels sure of herself and advise her on how best to present her work history. Call your local United Way chapter or the Federal Employment Development Department for more information. Local communities also sponsor job corps centers, some of which are specially tailored for women or young adults. Churches and synagogues frequently provide resources for job hunters, too. A good place to start looking is the community services or federal government section in your phone book.

Some dependent daughters are nervous about explaining why they've been out of work for so long. Job counselors may have some suggestions as to how to handle this, but if nothing else, your daughter can simply state that there was a family crisis (which is true). Besides, with the recent fluctuations in the economy, lots of people have been out of work for months or even years. If your daughter is punctual, pleasant, and seems eager to do the job, sooner or later someone will hire her despite the gap in her resumé.

To get your daughter started down the interview road, have her make the phone calls to United Way or the city job corps herself—don't do it for her. Even the most paralyzed daughter can dial a number and set up an appointment. If she doesn't have a car or if you think she might duck out at the last minute, offer to drive her to and from the meetings. Once she's enrolled in a program, there will be someone besides Mom urging her on to the next step—actually applying for a job.

"I Don't Have a Car, the Right Clothes, a Good Haircut . . ."

You, Mom, may have to pony up the money for these items. The car is the biggest sticking point. In some towns public transportation will suffice, but urban sprawl is a very real obstacle in most cities. Your daughter may legitimately need a vehicle, but ideally the car should not be purchased until she has a job. Until then, lend her your car, drive her to the interviews yourself, have her take the bus or a cab, or let her borrow a friend's car.

Once you know what your daughter's salary is going to be, you can help her make an educated decision about the type of car she can afford. If you're loaning her the money rather than buying her the car outright, add the details of that transaction to the independence contract.

The Endless Crisis

The endless crisis is a phenomenon I've noticed in some daughters when they first move out of Mom's house. Their anxieties go into overdrive, as Jennifer, sixty-five, discovered:

> My daughter finally moved out. She calls twice a day and has not stopped complaining. Her apartment is too hot, the people upstairs play their radio too loudly, her temp agency hasn't called with day work, she's lonely, she has a toothache, she has cramps, she hates Culver City, and on and on. She only left two weeks ago and she's still driving me crazy. I'm tempted to change my phone number and move without a forwarding address.

When a daughter moves into her own apartment, her main access to Mom is the telephone. It's not unusual for a dependent daughter to call three or four times a day with a laundry list of disasters. Most will be minor, but now and then a real crisis does occur.

The minor complaints can be dealt with fairly easily, if you can keep your own anxieties and frustration under control and stay calm and focused during the conversation. When your daughter tells you her problem, acknowledge it and then toss it back into her court: "Wow, you really have a problem. How are you going to handle it?" She'll claim not to know how to handle it—that's why she's calling you. But she'll find you surprisingly close-mouthed. You might ask her to list her options and then help her choose one, but my advice is to let her figure it out for herself. Don't play Ann Landers with her, no matter how helpless she behaves. After twenty minutes maximum, end the call, and do not talk to her more than once a day.

The success of this method hinges on your ability to control the call. That means controlling yourself during the conversation, limiting the amount of time you spend on each call, and sometimes resisting the urge to answer the phone altogether. Chapter nine, "Mom Power," includes a section on taming the telephone. Up until now you may have been a slave to it, answering every ring as faithfully as Pavlov's dog. Henceforth, you will be the master. *You* will decide how much complaining you feel like listening to; *you* will set the boundaries and enforce them. The methods in chapter nine work extremely well when dealing with an "endless crisis" daughter. It does require some willpower, but most moms manage to rise to the occasion.

The serious crisis is another matter. It's wise to have some sort of rainy-day fund with which to bail out your daughter should she need brakes for the car, emergency dental care, or another vital service. This fund should not be part of the independence contract; it's something you keep to yourself. Your daughter doesn't need to know that you're ready to pick up the pieces every now and then—otherwise, she'll fall apart every week. But be prepared to assist her in a legitimate crisis, as you would any child.

If She Won't Get Moving, Get Mad

Every now and then I encounter cases where the dependent daughter simply will not budge from her mother's house. Three, four, five months into the program, she's still camped out in the living room, deaf to Mom's pleas and suggestions. If your daughter hasn't made any forward motion two weeks after signing the contract, get mad. Don't let the process drag on while you deliberate over the best way to motivate her and avoid her nasty temper. The time for making nice is over; she's not doing her part. So take off the kid gloves.

Make clear to your daughter that, six weeks after signing the contract, you will box up her essential belongings, place them outside your front door, and change the locks. If you've followed the standard contract, your daughter should have found an apartment within a month. Since you are paying the first three months' rent, she doesn't have an excuse for not moving. If she doesn't want your help in searching for the apartment, so be it. Let her know from the moment she signs the contract that you will not go house hunting *for* her, although you'll be happy to do it *with* her. If she has not found housing within six weeks, she'll need to start calling her friends, because the free ride at Motel Mom is over.

Remind your daughter that the dates on the independence contract do not float. That is, the three months' rent you offered to pay apply to three *specific* months. She can't go flop at a friend's house for six months, then call you up and expect to carry on with the contract. If she stays with a friend for a month and then finds an apartment, she'll get the two remaining months' rent paid by you. If she doesn't find her own housing until three or four months down the line, you'll still adhere to the timetable set in the contract. The contract must have some teeth in it, or your daughter will just see it as an open-ended meal ticket to be used any time she pleases. That won't provide the incentive she needs to be self-sufficient *now,* which is the goal of this weaning process.

If your daughter does find another rescuer but approaches you in six months or a year and wants to resume the contract's program, you'll need to draft a new contract that takes into account her current circumstances. I'll discuss this process at the end of the chapter. Meanwhile, while you're still in the beginning weeks of the program, do not mention this option to your daughter.

Pats on the Back

With any luck at all, you won't have to spend the entire nine-month program in the role of merciless commandant. As soon as your daughter begins to make progress, you can be there to encourage her.

Cards, memos, messages on her answering machine—all of these will give your daughter strength as she eases into her new routine. Tell her that you appreciate the effort she's making: "You're doing great. Thank you for helping. I'm so glad you understand." Don't be surprised if she doesn't acknowledge these messages; during the transition from dependency to autonomy your daughter might be very angry with you. Try to find it in your heart to send these encouraging missives anyway. Later she may confess how much they meant to her, but even if she doesn't, offering your support is the compassionate thing to do. As her mom, you're always setting an example, and now is an especially good time to show your daughter how a loyal, loving mother behaves.

She's Leaving Home

Dependent daughters vary greatly in their response to the independence program. Some rage a lot and distance themselves from the parents whom they believe should have taken care of them forever. Others go through a mourning period and a spell of separation anxiety, but within several months begin to enjoy their new freedom. Most daughters have at least one close friend they can turn to for support during this time, when they no longer want to confide in Mom and Dad.

And then there are the daughters who immediately call every friend and relative they have, railing against the awful parents who threw them out. All too often, they find another rescuer to take over the dole. The dependent daughter expertly manipulates her new sponsor until that person begins to feel exploited; then she moves on to her next host. The pattern may continue for years, in which case her parents can at least be thankful that they are no longer at their daughter's mercy.

It's the rare daughter who falls right into line, thanks her mom and dad for their wisdom, and strides bravely out into the world. Far more common are rage, resistance, and a slow, hard climb back to normalcy. Think of the process as a long-term investment, not a quick fix. Within three or four years most families have regained their balance and most daughters are back on cordial terms with their mothers.

Whose Life Is at Stake, Yours or Hers?

During the first few months of the contract, you can expect your daughter to struggle against the program, to be spiteful and rude to you, or to stop talking to you altogether. This behavior is typical, designed to break down your resolve. Moms must prepare themselves for the onslaught of ill will, but they need to be equally aware of their own motives and emotions during this time. Believe it or not, many moms (and dads) sabotage their daughters just when they're about to make real progress.

The biggest culprit is Mom's old nemesis, fear. Now that her daughter is fighting mad, Mom's worst nightmares return: *My daughter won't love me anymore. How can I do this to her? I'm all by myself now; she'll never speak to me again. She's finally abandoning me. I'm making a mistake. What's so wrong about a mother and daughter living together forever?*

Every so often you read one of those stories about the mother and daughter who've gone and done it—they've lived together their whole lives long. They dwell in a dark, rundown house, where they collect newspapers and cats. They are each other's best friend; for the two of them, the rest of the world doesn't exist. Their relationship is symbiotic. And perhaps it's not so bad, if it's what they both want.

Is it what you want?

Mothers and daughters are not usually cut out to be each other's best friend. Even the most well-intentioned of them become antagonistic and resentful when they live under the same roof for too long, especially when it's Mom's roof. There's bound to be a power struggle, that moment when the daughter announces, "Your magazines are taking over the living room," and Mom replies, "Oh really? Well it's my living room, and if I want to pile magazines in it, that's exactly what I'll do." When it stops working and the two of you start fighting, it's time to differentiate.

At five A.M., when you toss and turn or sit alone at the kitchen table worrying about your daughter, you may wonder if you really had to separate from her. Ninety-nine percent of the time, the answer is yes. Just as you can't protect her from life, neither can she protect you. She wasn't put here to be your permanent companion. She, and you, must make separate lives for yourselves.

It's not just the loss of companionship that makes moms question their decision to free their dependent daughter. Sometimes both parents lose their nerve, caving in to their daughter's pleas just before she's ready to move out. Their underlying motive often has to do with their relationship with each other. If the problem child has been consuming most of their attention for a few years, it effectively takes the parents' focus off their own marriage. The daughter is a unifying factor, a common challenge. The rifts that might exist between Mom and Dad take a backseat to the more immediate crisis, their daughter. Once that problem goes away, Mom and Dad will have to look at each other again without distractions. For some couples, that's a frightening prospect.

Other couples use their dependent daughter as part of their ongoing battle with each other. They angle for her allegiance and involve her in their personal combat; in return, she gets free rent and board. A situation this dysfunctional obviously requires a counselor, not a book. But if you sense elements of this dynamic in your own family, step back and ask yourself, What is best for my daughter?

What's best for her is also what's best for you—a separate, distinct life, with the opportunity to grow and develop other relationships. The two of you should be able to enjoy true intimacy with each other, not the false closeness of rescuer and victim. Whose life will improve when you let your daughter go? Both hers and yours.

Preparing Yourself for Her Freedom

Whether or not the intimacy between you and your daughter was genuine, when she leaves your home (or begins to draw back from her dependent position) there will be a void in your life. It's wise to prepare yourself for this change by doing some homework of your own. I passionately believe in volunteer community work for older citizens who have the time and skills to spare. Newspapers often publish lists of organizations seeking volunteers, and houses of worship always have access to such information. Whether it's reading novels to blind people, helping teachers in a classroom, planting trees, or building houses with Habitat for Humanity, the list of opportunities is endless. The rewards will astonish you, I promise. In place of the upsetting, histrionic scenes with your daughter, you'll forge new friendships based on giving of yourself to people who legitimately need your help.

If you are married, the transition period as your daughter begins life on her own is the ideal time for you and your husband to take a vacation. Once she's past the first few weeks of frantic readjustment, take off. Get to know each other again, and try to not talk about your daughter too much. Take a car trip to a national park, or go on a cruise. Putting some physical distance between you and your daughter can be a tonic to the soul. This is equally true if you're not married, of course. Treat yourself to one of the many fascinating tours available in the United States and abroad—Elder Hostel is a terrific organization that offers seniors an economical way to travel in a safe group setting. Buy yourself whatever fun and relaxation you can afford, preferably far away from a telephone. You've earned it.

Renegotiating the Contract

As you work your way toward the final months of the independence contract, some of the questions you had at the outset will resolve themselves. At first the big issues, such as having your daughter move into her own apartment or get a job, will consume most of your attention. Along the way you'll probably make some compromises; for most mothers and daughters, the contract is a tug-of-war. Your daughter may fulfill some of her promises but ignore others, out of lack of will or sheer orneriness. That's all right—it's to be expected. If you accomplish the big milestones, you can both congratulate yourselves.

With the large obstacles out of the way, you'll need to consider what to do once the nine-month contract is up. Most parents renegotiate the contract by drafting a new version that reflects the changing relationship with their daughter. This time around, parents can afford to pay more attention to their own needs. In the first contract, the main goal was to help your daughter become self-sufficient. Now you'll lay the groundwork for a healthy, equitable long-term relationship with her. From this point on, the contract should offer the parents some gratification, too.

Selena and Richard, both in their early sixties, had been supporting their daughter Tammy for years when they came to me for help. We wrote an independence contract that took into account Tammy's borderline depressive personality disorder. She could hold down a low-stress, low-paying job but might always require some support from her parents.

Tammy's eleven-year-old son, Josh, added another element to the dynamic. A bright child, mature beyond his years, he had assumed a near-parenting role with his mother. Josh loved spending time with his grandparents—he could be a boy with them, not a miniature adult. Tammy, Selena, and Richard all adored Josh, but during the term of the first contract, Tammy reneged on her promise to let him visit Selena and Richard.

"She's very pissed off at us," Selena told me. "But she wants us to keep paying part of her rent and Josh's school tuition.

> She refuses to speak to us and grabs the phone out of
> Josh's hand if he's talking to me. She makes herself and
> Josh unavailable, without ever coming out and openly
> refusing to let us see him. She has kept her word about
> holding down a job, but we never see her, never celebrate
> family occasions together, and I haven't visited with my
> grandson in three months.

Prior to writing the independence contract, Selena and Richard had been fearful about saying no to Tammy. Nine months later, as the contract came to an end, they were less frightened. Tammy was being disagreeable, but it was clear that she wasn't going to skip town with Josh and that she still needed their financial aid to the point where it gave them some clout. They had also begun to realize that the person they were most concerned about for the time being was Josh, not Tammy.

Selena and Richard drafted a new contract. In exchange for their continued rent and tuition payments, they would get to see Josh twice a month for an overnight visit at their house. Since Tammy didn't want to speak to her parents, they would pick Josh up from school on Friday and drop him off at his house Sunday morning, without interacting with Tammy in any way. Tammy would be spared seeing Selena and Richard, and Josh would be able to spend time with them. If Tammy interfered with the visit, she wouldn't get the financial aid.

I've found this approach to be very useful when dealing with angry daughters who deny visitation to the grandparents as a form of punishment. By promising not to interact with your daughter, you avoid an ugly confrontation when you visit with your grandchild. It's an excellent way to reduce the stress of the situation for everyone, including the child.

Each time you draft a new contract, reevaluate your circumstances. For most parents, it makes sense to draft a contract either every six months or every year, depending on their daughter's progress. Look over the wish list you wrote in chapter three and think about the expectations you have of your daughter. Are they realistic, and do they make sense at this stage of her differentiation from you?

As she regains her independence, your daughter may want to distance herself from you more than you'd like. You may find yourself tempted to lure her back with a monetary bribe built into the revised contract. For instance, you might offer to buy her some new furniture in exchange for more visits. If you do this, you're going right back to the money-for-love trade-off that made your daughter dependent in the first place. Instead, accept your daughter's distance for now. Many daughters need to miss

Mom before they can appreciate her, so give your daughter that chance. When you're renegotiating the contract, aim for a balance between what feels fair to you and what your daughter needs to continue making progress.

If the First Contract Didn't Fly, Try Again Later

Sometimes you have to draft a new independence contract because the first contract never jelled. This happens if a dependent daughter distances herself from her parents and finds another rescuer, but later comes back to Mom and Dad for a second chance at the contract. In that case, you'll write a new contract that takes into account her existing circumstances. If she has already moved out of your house, don't let her move back in! Appeal to the current rescuer to let your daughter stay there until she can find other housing (you might offer to pay the rescuer rent). If the person refuses, and you can afford it, put your daughter up in a month-to-month furnished apartment while she looks for a permanent residence.

Capitalize on whatever support system your daughter has pulled together while she was estranged from you, be it government aid, food stamps, or a part-time job. Include all these factors in the new independence contract. And don't be surprised if your daughter is just as sullen now as she was when she marched out of your house all those months ago. Chances are she hasn't seen the error of her ways, but has come back to you as a last resort. Still, as long as she seems to be acting in good faith, try to work something out with her. In the long run her self-sufficiency will be worth it to both of you.

A year or two from now, you and your daughter may decide that you no longer need a contract to maintain your relationship.

If all goes well, the concepts of independence, honesty, and personal responsibility will become second nature to you both. As separate, equal adults, you can then build a lasting friendship based on love and respect. I've been there, I've seen many women go through it successfully, and I wish you good luck!

PART THREE

THE DISSATISFIED

DAUGHTER

CHAPTER SEVEN

Got an Hour, Mom?
I Just Called to Complain

The calls come in around the same time every day, when she has a break at the office. The litany starts with, "If you only knew how much I hate this job," and from there she goes on to her weight, her husband, her health, her friends. I keep asking, "How can I help? What can I do?" She just keeps complaining. Am I always supposed to be sad like her, so our feelings match? I'm her opposite: I'm content. How did I get her for a daughter?

—Annette, age sixty-five

"*I* JUST WANT HER TO BE HAPPY." ALL MOTHERS SAY IT, and we've all watched and winced as our daughters made decisions that were dangerous or dumb. But for the mother of a dissatisfied daughter, her girl's quest for happiness becomes a lifelong curse. A dissatisfied daughter is unpleasable; she will never be happy. *Dissatisfied* is actually a gentle way to describe this type of woman. She is disagreeable, irritable, whiny. She flares up at the least provocation. She is a chronic complainer. She is the one for whom nothing seems to go right. She brings down the birthday party—even Grandma doesn't want to see her.

Nearly half the mothers I counsel are plagued with dissatisfied daughters. A mother becomes deeply troubled when her daughter is unhappy, and she usually responds by trying to solve the daughter's problem. But Mom cannot, and never will be able to, make her dissatisfied daughter happy. Only the daughter can do that. No matter what advice, money, or support Mom offers, it's never enough, and she is doomed to feel like a failure.

You can't fix your dissatisfied daughter, but the good news is, you can improve your relationship with her. Even if she doesn't change, you can, and that will make a tremendous difference in the quality of your life. In this chapter I'll explain some possible reasons for your daughter's unpleasable personality, and I'll describe the ways you may have become enmeshed in her dissatisfaction. In chapters eight and nine, I'll show you how to retool your relationship with her, regardless of her happiness quotient.

The "Lucy" Syndrome

One of cartoonist Charles Schultz's most humorous creations is Lucy, the perennially crabby girl. Always ill-tempered, she runs roughshod over the other children and metes out harsh psychological advice from her five-cent therapy booth. Everyone tiptoes around her to avoid her bad moods. That's the way it is with disagreeable people; the rest of us work overtime to keep the peace with them. But it's not so funny when "Lucy" is your own offspring.

If you are the mother of a dissatisfied daughter, your shoes are probably worn thin from all the tiptoeing you've done over the years. You may have prayed for the day she'd leave home, assuming that things would improve once she was grown. But the dissatisfied daughter is often just as unhappy as an adult as she was when she was a teenager. Most have been irritable since childhood. They have a hard time getting along with everyone, not just Mom. They fight with their brothers and sisters, their friends, their boyfriends.

A favorite theme of the dissatisfied daughter is her bad luck: "Things don't work out for me. Why can't I ever get a break?" Or she blames other people for the disappointments in her life: "Why are all guys so commitment-phobic? If I could find someone who wasn't a jerk, maybe I could have a good relationship." It's never her fault. Dissatisfied daughters sometimes have an inflated sense of entitlement, a belief that the world owes them the best seat in the restaurant, the most understanding boss, a car that never breaks down. When things don't go just right for them, they fume, rant, and make life miserable for those around them.

Who bears the brunt of the dissatisfied daughter's gripe with the world? Her mother. The daughter may be unpleasant to other people, but other people will only put up with so much. Mom will put up with just about anything. She internalizes her daughter's unhappiness, taking it on as her own. And because she is helpless to make things better for her girl, the relationship can become a grueling, extremely stressful experience for Mom.

Moms often tell me how frustrated they are by their helplessness, but accepting that helplessness is the way out of the dilemma. Until now, you've been held hostage by your daughter's discontent—unable to ease it, yet doomed to bear witness to it whenever she calls or visits. You may have assumed that the only solution is to somehow arrange for your daughter to be happy so she'll stop complaining. That viewpoint puts all the power in your daughter's hands. Fortunately there are other ways to deal with her, but in order to feel comfortable with them you need some insight into her behavior.

Life with the Terminally Crabby

The world is full of crabby people. If the crab is your friend, coworker, or even your sibling, you learn to deal with it or you curtail your contact with that person. If the crab is your boss, you quit. If it's your husband, you go to a counselor or, in the worst-case scenario, a divorce lawyer. But if the crabby one is your child, the emotional waters are much murkier.

Leslie, a tall, easygoing woman of fifty-eight, was the mother of Wendy, twenty-seven. Despite Wendy's outward successes, she was not a happy camper, and she let Leslie know it on a regular basis. "She complains constantly," Leslie told me, "and I often wonder if she will ever find happiness in this world.

> She has a wonderful life, children and a committed husband, plus a beautiful home and lots of money. Yet she is never satisfied with her trips, her health, her volunteer job, her looks. She complains about me, too. I am too confident, I act superior, I intimidate her.

"How does she act around other people?" I queried.

"Well," replied Leslie, "she's never been very cheerful. Her brother and sister used to call her The Pill."

"And now?"

"They don't see her much," Leslie admitted.

"How often do you see her?" I asked.

"Once a week. We get together Thursday nights for dinner. We have a favorite restaurant, so we always go there to catch up."

"Do you enjoy it?" I asked.

It took Leslie a long time to reply. Finally she said, "I don't know. I can't say I enjoy it. It's something we do—she expects it."

"What do you talk about? What do you 'catch up' on?"

"Her life," Leslie said wryly, "and what's wrong with it."

As it turned out, Thursday nights weren't the only time Leslie heard about Wendy's disappointing life. Wendy called daily to report on all the minor inconveniences and injustices dealt her. The conversations, whether in person or over the telephone, usually ended with Wendy insulting her mother or picking a fight with her. Leslie's frustration with Wendy echoed that of many mothers: "If she dislikes me so much, why does she keep calling me? If she doesn't want my advice, why does she keep telling me her problems? What does she want from me?"

The daily phone calls, the need to unload on Mom, the problems that Mom can never adequately solve, all are typical of the dissatisfied daughter. While Mom may understand her daughter's need to vent, it's harder to make sense of the daughter's rude, even abusive, behavior toward her. Yes, she's naturally irritable and knows Mom will put up with it, but in many instances it feels more personal than that: the daughter seems to actively dislike her mother. In which case, why does she call so often?

I believe the dissatisfied daughter's motive is an intense, unconscious need to connect with her mother, regardless of the tenor of that connection. She may not approve of her mother, appreciate her, or treat her with respect, but she needs frequent contact with Mom the same way a baby needs the breast.

Just like their dependent sisters, dissatisfied daughters need Mom's support far in excess of what a well-adjusted daughter would need. Unlike dependent daughters, however, dissatisfied women are functional in everyday society. They hold jobs, have families, and appear to be relatively healthy, if grumpy, adults. But scratch the surface, and all is not well. They have not quite made it in the adult world; they haven't formed a mature, independent identity. Dissatisfied daughters need steady nurturance from Mom, but they can't articulate this need. Instead, they often reverse it. "Mom expects me to call her every day," a dissatisfied daughter will complain; later, her mother will pull me aside and say, "I don't want her to call so much. Can you please ask her to stop?"

The desire for daily contact with Mother is unusual in an adult, but there's nothing wrong with it if it makes both women happy. For mothers of dissatisfied daughters, this is not the case. The complaining phone call may alleviate some of her daughter's anxiety, but it's a dreaded event for Mom. It's not just that the news is always bad, which would be dreary enough. It's that when a mother listens to her daughter's problems, she instinctively tries to solve them.

Why No Solution Is the Right Solution

"My daughter is always annoyed with me," said Pam, fifty-six.

> It seems that I invariably step on her toes about personal things in her life. She tells me she is in debt, so I advise her on how to save money. She tells me she needs clothes, so I point out the bargain shops I frequent. She said she needed some dental work, so I called the USC dental school to get her into their intern-practice program. She really flipped over that one! I was only trying to help.

A particularly baffling aspect of the dissatisfied daughter's behavior is her steadfast rejection of Mom's advice—*even though she keeps telling Mom her problems.* No matter what solution her mother offers, the daughter will usually veto it with a "Yes, but . . ." response. So why seek out Mom in the first place?

The answer is, sympathy. The dissatisfied daughter doesn't want you to solve her problems, she wants you to feel sorry for her. I've questioned many daughters about this need for sympathy; Faith, thirty-six, was especially enlightening on the topic. I asked her, "When you tell your mother your problems, are you looking for her pity?"

"Oh, no," answered Faith. "Not pity."

"But you're coming across as pathetic," I said.

"I'm not pathetic. I just want sympathy. I just want her to understand me."

And that's the link. Sympathy, to many dissatisfied daughters, equals understanding, and understanding equals love. If she were a different personality type, she'd use another tack to win Mom's affection. Some daughters, for example, try to secure Mom's favor by being the "good girl," always there at Mother's beck and call. The dissatisfied daughter sees the world in a gloomier light. The coin of her realm is problems and complaints—that's all she has to bring to the table. She seeks to trade them for your love, not your bargain-hunting tips.

Once you recognize your daughter's need for contact and sympathy, you can respond to her problems by being empathetic and validating her indignation over the day's crisis—in other words, by providing some harmless, nonintrusive commiseration. In chapter nine I'll explain the technique in detail; for now, the point to remember is that most of the time, your daughter doesn't really want you to solve her problems, so you can stop trying.

Mom-Bashing

Recognizing your daughter's emotional needs can help you understand her prickly behavior, but some daughters take nastiness to an unacceptable extreme. When the brush-offs, cruel comments, and disrespectful attitude escalate past the annoying point, there's no excuse for it, no matter how unhappy your daughter is. I call this sort of abuse "mom-bashing," and from what I've seen in my mother-daughter sessions, it's becoming epidemic. Dissatisfied daughters are among the worst offenders. They've got a sour temperament anyway, and Mom is an easy target.

"I can't ever please her," a mom will tearfully confide to me. Well, no, you can't. A mom-bashing daughter will criticize everything about you. She'll disapprove of your friends, the way you spend your money, the color of your hair. "You're still bowling?" she'll demand. "You're still playing bridge? What are you doing with those people? How can you stand doing those things?" Yet if you changed your activities it would make no difference. She'd be critical no matter what you did.

When searching for a method to her meanness, realize that your daughter's displeasure with you is very likely a projection of her displeasure with herself. She is not content, and she doesn't want you to be content either. She doesn't feel happy or adequate, so she'd like you to feel unhappy and inadequate too. In psychological terms, this is called *twinning*.

In Part I, I described how a mother often expects her grown daughter to be a duplicate of her and how this expectation can spoil a potentially healthy friendship between the two of them. Daughters also want to see themselves reflected in their mother. They want Mom to match them in mood, style, tastes, and worldviews. If a dissatisfied daughter is intolerant, fastidious, and dresses like a nun, she may desire Mom to do the same. If her mother is relatively content, easygoing, and dresses flamboyantly, the daughter will chafe at the disparity between them. The most infuriating difference, from the daughter's perspective, is her mother's sense of well-being.

Dissatisfied daughters can be intensely envious of their mothers, especially if Mom is successful in areas where the daughter feels inadequate. Molly, seventy-one, was astonished to learn the extent of her daughter's envy. Natalie, thirty-seven, was a highly regarded law professor with lots of friends, a job at a top university, and lifetime security. As proud as Molly was of her daughter, she had begun to distance herself from Natalie because the younger woman was so unpleasant and critical of her parents. In private sessions with Natalie, I finally learned the reason: she envied her mother's forty-five-year marriage to her dad. As successful as she was, Natalie's own marraige had crumbled after just five years. She didn't feel successful and secure; she felt lonely and panicked. Seeing her happy parents only intensified her fear of growing old alone, and she took it out on her mother.

Mom-bashing isn't limited to dissatisfied daughters. Some families have an ugly tradition of insulting Mom, which the children often learn at Daddy's knee. If your husband treats you disrespectfully, it's no wonder your children do the same. Isolated in the little universe of the household, a mom can get used to being the scapegoat. If everyone in your family is beating up on you, you need to get into a support group or schedule some sessions with a therapist. No book can give you the kind of hands-on help you need, and this book in particular is aimed at mother-daughter relationships, not wider family dynamics. If you're feeling the sting of an unkind family, the suggestions in chapter eight can aid you in recovering some of your self-respect and setting boundaries. But I urge you not to rely on those suggestions alone— instead, talk to a professional counselor who can give you some perspective on your situation.

Taking It Like a Mom

"You're my therapist of last resort," Jane joked as she settled into my office on her first visit. Sixtyish and comfortably plump, Jane appeared determined to laugh about her predicament. Her daughter Lisa, thirty-three, had been distraught and angry for a long time, but over the last two years she had pulled her parents ever deeper into her unhappiness.

> Lisa insists that her father and I have a lot of problems and need therapy. We agreed to accompany her for some joint sessions to see if we could ameliorate her hostility to us. We also paid for the therapy. At first it was the three of us, then Lisa and her dad, then Lisa and me. Can you imagine twenty-four weeks of her dumping on us? And she's still hostile! She is so unhappy with her life and her relationships that she projects all her negative feelings out on us, and we are exhausted.

Jane had come to me after breaking off with Lisa's therapist, although she continued to pay for Lisa's private sessions. Doing it Lisa's way hadn't worked, and now Jane was out of ideas.

Jane was not unusual in her willingness to do anything to ease her daughter's pain. Unfortunately, most mothers have no guidelines on how to handle their unhappy adult daughters. Whether their daughter is a mom-basher or merely a relentless kvetch, moms typically follow the same well-worn, futile paths of response. In so doing, they sign on for a lifelong sentence of failure and fatigue.

First, as I mentioned earlier, the mom tries to solve her daughter's problems by offering advice that the daughter routinely rejects. Another approach is to try to make the daughter's boo-boos better by buying her a little happiness. This is a natural impulse for mothers, one that probably began forty thousand years ago around the first campfire ("You burned your finger? Here, have an extra antelope morsel"). When our girls were young, we'd soothe their hurts with hugs, food, or little treats. A hurt child got a bit of extra attention. The dissatisfied daughter is in a constant state of hurt, and the frustrated mom often resorts to bribery to ease her daughter's pain—and to buy herself a precious day or two of silence.

Unlike the dependent daughter, the dissatisfied daughter is not usually angling for a payoff, at least not consciously. Her distress is genuine, and the bribes don't ease it for long. Mom may ask, "If I buy you a new coat, will it make you feel better?" "Yeah, I guess so," the daughter will concede. Mom will pull out her checkbook, guiltily hoping that the shopping trip will keep her daughter busy for a while. In time, the daughter comes to expect the payoff. But the check is cold comfort; her problems can't be solved by a new toy anymore.

Moms are often unaware that they are writing those checks to satisfy themselves, not their daughters. So I tell them about a simple way to stay aware of their motives: At the bottom of every check is a little line marked "Memo." If every time you wrote a check to your daughter, you had to fill in that line with the appropriate word—"guilt," "payoff," "bribe," "shut up," "enough, already"—you'd quickly realize what you are doing, how much it's costing, and how ineffective it is. If check writing worked, there would be an end in sight. Is there?

Time and water will wear down any stone. Time and an unhappy daughter's complaints can wear down the strongest mom, until she no longer lives her own inner life but instead is drawn along in her daughter's emotional slipstream. When her advice keeps getting rejected and the payoffs buy less and less peace, a mom will sometimes simply cave in. She'll go into mourning. With every setback her daughter suffers, the mother will become more depressed. She'll begin to identify with her daughter's problems as if the problems were her own. Such a mother loses herself to her daughter's misery, but even that is not enough to change the daughter. Mom's sacrifice is irrelevant, a complete waste.

When a mother like this seeks out my help, my first job is to make her understand that she and her daughter must separate and handle their problems individually. I lay it on the line: "You have permission to put away your guilt, your checkbook, your payoffs, your mourning apparatus. Take off the black veil and start walking, because you're not going to do this anymore. It's not good for you."

What About the Guilt?

"Put away your guilt." So easy to say, so hard for a mother to do. Guilt is a camouflage feeling: it hides other emotions that a mom considers shameful. All those unacceptable feelings—your dislike of your daughter, your urge to avoid her, your wish that she were more like your other children, your attempts to shut her up by writing checks—get translated into guilt.

Take the likability issue. In *The Lion in Winter,* Eleanor of Aquitaine put it to her husband bluntly: "Henry, I have a confession . . . I don't much like our children." Ah, the release of simply being able to say it out loud! But many moms can't admit to themselves that while they will always love their daughter, they don't much like her. Even thinking it floods them with guilt.

Guilt about failing your daughter—not providing the right advice, not "being there" for her, and so on—usually masks anger. *Why should I have to solve all your problems?* you may want to scream. *But she's your daughter. If you won't help her, who will?* replies the perfect mom you think you ought to be. The myths of motherhood decree that you are duty-bound to support your children, no matter what. There's no room for anger, no question as to who is really failing, you or your daughter.

But the most insidious type of guilt is that which masks your fear that you created the monster, that somehow, lurking amid the balanced meals, ballet lessons, and tooth fairy prizes, was a message that your daughter was not good enough. Did you wound your daughter? Is she correct in her criticisms of you? Is it all your fault?

Born on the Wrong Side of the Bed

If you were my client, we could sit down together and gain some insight into how much, if anything, your parenting style had to do with your daughter's present incapacity for happiness. Some parents do put a damper on their children's potential for enjoyment by punishing them for boisterous, exuberant behavior. The children then may become conditioned to suppress joyous feelings. If yours was a very strict household where high spirits were frowned upon, it's possible that your daughter has reacted to that environment by developing *anhedonia,* the inability to experience pleasure.

But anhedonia can just as easily occur in people who were brought up in an average, nonrepressive household. The condition is sometimes, but not always, related to depression, and it may well be caused by a combination of genetics and social environment. Family environment can play a part, but unless your daughter was abused or raised in a rigid, joyless home, it is highly unlikely that your parenting style caused your daughter's grouchiness.

Moms who have several children are more readily convinced

of this than mothers of a single dissatisfied daughter. When there are three siblings and only one is irritable, Mom can assume that since everyone else turned out okay, she must have been doing something right. But given a mother's natural tendency to worry and blame herself, it's worth stepping back for a few moments and looking at the happiness question in a context larger than your immediate family.

For the past thirty years, psychologists have been researching people's potential for happiness. When tackling the nature-or-nurture aspect of the issue, twins provide important clues. Behavioral geneticist David Lykken and psychologist Auke Tellegen, both of the University of Minnesota, studied more than thirteen hundred sets of twins, some identical, some fraternal. The identical twins, who have matching genes, expressed nearly identical levels of happiness whether they were raised in the same family or separately. Fraternal twins, whose genes are about as similar as ordinary siblings, showed no such close correlation. This led the researchers to conclude that our potential for happiness may be at least partly genetically preset.

Society, too, has an impact on people's happiness. The World Values Survey, which has been monitoring the relative happiness of different countries since the 1960s, publishes a list of fifty countries ranked by the percentage of people who consider themselves "quite happy or very happy." The United States ranked thirteenth in 1996—about 88 percent of Americans claim they're happy. At the top of the list are the Scandinavian countries—Iceland is number one, followed by Sweden, Denmark, Norway, and the Netherlands. Ronald Inglehart, one of the survey's coordinators, postulates that these countries rank so highly because "they are small, manageable societies, homogeneous and prosperous, where life is predictable." Inglehart feels that society has more to do with people's happiness than genetics. Most researchers fall somewhere in between, believing that there probably is some sort of happiness set point for each individual but that its exact cause has yet to be pinned down.

You need only go to your corner bookstore to get a sense of how deeply the happiness issue matters to us—whole sections are devoted to books that promise to teach us how to find meaning in our lives and become happier. Some see it as a spiritual issue, some as a response to our rapidly changing culture. But can normal, loving parents unintentionally turn an amiable daughter into a disagreeable grumbler? Probably not. You just don't have that much power. No matter how guilty you feel, you didn't single-handedly create your daughter's temperament.

Regardless of the reasons why your daughter is so discontent, the bottom line is that you have been dancing to her unhappy tune for too long. If you honestly feel that you may have played a role in her psychological problems, the best option for both of you is to seek the help of a professional therapist, either together or separately. You each need to understand the other's perception of your family history and then move on from there.

If, on the other hand, your home life was about average—not without its galling moments, but not without joy, either—you need to ask yourself the following: If my daughter was simply born with an irritable disposition, what sort of relationship do I want to have with her from now on?

She May Never Change— but You Can Change Your Relationship

I believe that everyone can change if they want to, including your unhappy daughter. But if she does decide to readjust her outlook on life, it probably won't be because you talked her into it. You cannot change her. You cannot make her happy. And, sad to say, a good number of dissatisfied daughters never do change. You have to be prepared for that possibility and plan your future accordingly.

Back in chapter three I asked you to write a wish list, where you set down all the things you wanted in your relationship with your daughter. Read it again now, and with each item, ask yourself if you'd still include that wish if your daughter did not modify her personality. Do you still want "more visits with her" if she's always going to be unpleasant? Do you want her to "be happier"? Or to "stop complaining"? Amend your list so that it only reflects what's actually possible. Maybe she can't be happier, and maybe you can't get her to stop complaining entirely, but you can control the amount of time you spend listening to her complaints and witnessing her unhappiness. To a great degree, you can set the tone of your visits and phone calls with her. You can take the lead in your dance with her—in chapters eight and nine, I'll show you how.

CHAPTER EIGHT

Changing the Rules

Before, it was as if my daughter and I were from different planets. We couldn't kid around like I do with my other children; we each misconstrued what the other said. I was afraid of my daughter, and she was hypersensitive. Everything was perceived as an insult or judgment.

These days the angry tension has diminished a lot. I've learned how to be honest with her. She may not always like it, but things feel much more calm.

—Benecia, age fifty-five

ALL FAMILIES DEVELOP THEIR OWN LANGUAGE, A REPERtoire of stories, expressions, and inside jokes that weave the clan together. This verbal shorthand is a big part of what makes a family *familiar*, a refuge from the anonymous world outside. Mothers of dissatisfied daughters often report that this familiar territory is missing in their relationship with their daughters. Instead of speaking a common language, they consistently misunderstand each other. "It's like we're in separate orbits," a mother will explain, or "Talking to her is like walking through a minefield."

Turning the minefield into safe, neutral territory is the first step in creating a better relationship with your daughter. In order to do this, you'll need to honestly confront her about what's making her so unhappy and to tell her about your own feelings toward her—warts and all. In this chapter I'll show you how to accomplish this daunting task so you can set the stage for a new, more civilized friendship.

To the mom who has spent years tiptoeing around her daughter's bad moods, the idea of purposely confronting her is about as appealing as diving naked into a public swimming pool. In addition to the fact that they hate fighting with her, most moms are afraid of losing their daughter if they rock the boat. As I mentioned in chapter four, if you'd worked with hundreds of mothers and daughters as I have, you would know that it is extremely rare for a dependent or dissatisfied daughter to permanently cease contact with her mother. She may snub her and rage at her for a while, but ultimately she needs Mom as much as Mom needs her.

The techniques for change that I describe in this book are all based on the concept of measured honesty. Tell the truth, but tell it gently. Be tactful. At all times, do no harm. As you'll discover, my methods are not complicated machinations or outrageous formulas for living—but they are an approach that hasn't occurred to the average mom. If you stay committed to the process, it will change your relationship. Even if your daughter barely acknowledges what's happening, you'll experience a great shift in the quality of the time you spend together. And if she is enthusiastic about improving the relationship, who knows how far the two of you can go?

Daughter, What's Bothering You?

There's an old adage that says, "The only way out is through." This is especially true when it comes to your relationship with a dissatisfied daughter. To get out of the quagmire, you must work through it by asking her some tough questions, such as "Why are you so unhappy with your life?" and "Do you and I have a problem?" You'll need to be resilient enough to handle her answers and strong enough to tell her the truth about what's bothering *you*.

How do you approach your prickly daughter with a list of hot-button questions? Very gently. It's a good idea to write out the questions rather than ask them verbally; that way you can encourage her to think them over and talk to you later, or better yet, write the answers down. These questions should not be answered on the spur of the moment. They deserve to be pondered with as much seriousness as your daughter can muster.

Choose a time near the end of one of your visits to approach your daughter with your list of questions. You don't want to get into a big discussion with her before she's had time to look at the list; you just want to share your feelings with her. Be truthful, and try to keep the language low-key:

> I know it's hard for you to talk about this, and you and I are not on a very intimate level. But I've written down a few questions that I'd like you to answer at your leisure, because I'm really in a quandary. I'll never hold your answers against you, and when we talk about them later I hope you won't hold my words against me.
>
> I need to know what's bothering you. No matter what I say or do, it seems that you've always got an ax to grind. There's a tone in your voice that says that you're very dissatisfied with me about something. If I knew what was disturbing you, it would help me a lot. Right now I keep asking myself, "What did I do wrong?" If only I knew, perhaps I could try to make things better between us.
>
> I am unhappy with the way things are, and I sense that you're unhappy too. We need a new relationship, because the one we have right now isn't working. I'm getting older, and I love you, and I want to try to improve things while I still have some good years left.

It will take courage to say all this to your daughter. But you must recite this speech, or some version of it, in order to break the ice with her. Notice that you are not accusing her of anything other than being unhappy. Many mothers and daughters are on such shaky ground with each other that voicing this obvious truth—we are both unhappy—is terribly threatening. It's possible that your daughter won't be able to respond to your appeal other than to silently shake her head or utter something vague such as "I'm fine, Mother. Nothing's wrong." It's equally likely that she'll blow up and refuse to discuss anything with you. That's why you will hand her the list folded, so that she doesn't even have to look at it until she's safely out of your sight. A curious daughter might want to peek, but many won't read it until later.

The sample list below is composed of questions my clients have asked their daughters. These are quite general; you should reflect on the specific tender spots between you and your daughter and include them in your list as well. Think about the topics that are the most difficult for you two to discuss, such as "Are you angry with me because Dad died? Are you upset because your husband and I don't get along? Do you still think I love your brother more than I love you?"

As you compile your list, mentally rehearse what her answers might be and how you might respond to them. Remember: *measured honesty*. "Yes, I did always love your brother best—he was easier to get along with" is not measured honesty. Instead say, "I love you with all my heart, which is why I'm putting myself on the line here to make things better for us." Tell the truth, but do no harm.

The Hard Questions

- What do you want from our relationship?
- In your view, what is wrong about our relationship and what is right?
- What do I do that irritates you?

- What do I do that pleases you?
- Do you think I'm too intrusive?
- Do you think I offer too much advice?
- If you could have the ideal mother-daughter relationship, what would it be? What would be the boundaries?
- How can we change what we have now—what would you be willing to do, and what would you like me to do?

The Top Five Things You Do That Irritate Your Daughter

From the vantage point of many years in clinical practice, I can give you a sneak preview of how your daughter may answer some of the questions on your list. Forewarned is forearmed; the truth won't hurt so badly if you're prepared for it.

Each of the five irritating habits listed below spring from an innocent source—a mother's love for her daughter. Because you care so much about her, your curiosity and anxiety can override common sense and prudent boundaries. The unmet expectations you had for your daughter contribute to some of these bad habits; others are just typical mom stuff that an amiable daughter might shrug off but an irritable daughter finds intolerable.

Even if your daughter doesn't mention a single one of these habits, stop doing them. The results will amaze you.

1. Stop interrogating her. "So, what's going on? Whatcha doin'? How's the baby? How's the job? Did you get the carpets cleaned yet? Did you call the carpet guy I told you about?" It doesn't take a dissatisfied daughter to get peeved at an onslaught like this. Stop asking her so many questions, even though it goes against your impulse to make sure she's all right. (Of course, there's another less noble reason moms interrogate their daughters: nosiness.) The irritable daughter will usually respond to her mother's queries either by snapping, "None of your business!" or by launching into a thirty-minute complaint session. Neither is very satisfying for Mother.

It's pretty hard to have a conversation without asking any questions at all, but do try to resist prying into the workings of your daughter's everyday life. Unfortunately, even general queries such as "What's up with you?" can provoke free-floating anxiety in some daughters. How, then, can you find out if your daughter is OK without getting cursed at or dumped on?

When she is ready to talk about the list of questions you gave her, bring up the interrogation issue yourself (if she doesn't mention it first and it's relevant for you two). You might broach the subject like this:

> Sometimes I hear myself peppering you with questions and I get the feeling that it really annoys you. The truth is, I miss being close to you and I need to know that you're OK. I'm not expecting you to tell me the personal details of your life, but I don't see you all that often, so the only way I can find out about you is to ask. If I say, "What's going on?" and you say, "Nothing," then I feel as if I need to keep asking more questions.
>
> Let's do it differently from now on. If I start asking too many questions, instead of getting angry at me, maybe you could say, "Mom, everything is fine right now. If there's something happening that you need to know about, I promise I'll tell you." That will put my mind at ease, and we can move on to other topics.

Other topics, by the way, will be lighter topics. In chapter nine I'll describe how to master the art of light conversation; it's a crucial element in moving the relationship to a more enjoyable plane.

2. *Stop invading her privacy.* One of the reasons moms have such a tough time scaling back their questions is that they feel entitled to know every nook and cranny of their daughters' lives. Queries such as "What are you having for dinner tonight?" seem harmless enough, but piled one on top of another they become intrusive. And the invasion sometimes goes beyond mere questioning. There are moms who walk into a daughter's house and routinely open drawers, rifle through the mail, clean the kitchen, examine the contents of the medicine cabinet. No detail is too small to escape their notice or comment.

There is a poignancy to this sort of lust for details, as if the mothers are vampires living off the juice of their daughters' lives. More than one mother has confessed to me that she calls her daughter when she knows she isn't home, just to hear her voice on the answering machine! You'd expect this behavior from a stalker, not a mother.

So back off, Mom. Exercise the same restraint in your daughter's house as you would in the home of a friend. If she has made it clear to you that she doesn't want to discuss a particular subject, respect her wishes. You have the right to know if she's healthy, safe, and emotionally sound; other than that, it's her call. The same goes for her access to information about you.

3. *Stop judging her by the way you live.* The twentieth century—some mothers just can't get used to it. "When I was your age I didn't dye my hair," they'll admonish their daughters. "When I was a young mother I didn't have a housekeeper." "I've never owed money on a credit card in my life." "Plastic surgery? Are you out of your mind?" I'll repeat my favorite mantra: *You and your daughter are separate individuals.* In addition, the world is a different place than it was twenty or thirty years ago. It is inappropriate for you to judge your adult daughter by the way you live, and she has every right to resent you for it.

Whenever a judgmental comment begins to burble from your lips, stop and ask yourself, "What am I really worried about?" Many of these comments arise from a mom's instinct to protect her child; she doesn't want to see her daughter sink into debt or go under the surgeon's knife unnecessarily. But announcing "I would never consider a nose job!" sounds like a judgment, not a message of concern. Your daughter probably perceives it as an attempt to control her. Reframe your question so that it addresses what's really bothering you, as in, "I don't know much about cosmetic surgery, and I'm a little scared for you. Is there anything you can tell me about the procedure that might ease my mind?"

If you search your soul and find that you're not really concerned about your daughter's welfare but just want to "guide" her actions, hold your tongue.

4. Stop criticizing her for being innately different than you. Mom is conservative; daughter is a free spirit. Mom has a few close friends; daughter has dozens of pals. Mom is a bookworm; daughter lives for rock climbing and backpacking. Sometimes our daughters are similar to us in tastes and temperament, but very often they are not. As I've mentioned before, we all want to see ourselves reflected (and therefore validated) in other people, especially in our daughters. Many moms have never consciously considered the possibility that their daughters aren't wrong or rebellious, they're just their own person. All the criticism in the world cannot change their natural inclinations.

Criticizing your daughter for being innately different from you is not only futile, it's unkind. My hope is that after you do the exercises in the first three chapters of this book, you'll have a more realistic understanding of your daughter's personality. Accept her uniqueness and put an end to the criticism.

5. Stop giving her unsolicited advice. Here's a not-so-secret secret: We moms do know how to solve our daughters' problems. We're older, wiser, and have been there before. We really could straighten out their lives, if only they'd listen to us!

But they won't. They don't want our advice. Moms, take it from someone who's had this conversation with literally hundreds of women: Do not offer unsolicited advice. If you're itching to solve your daughter's problem, ask, "Do you want my advice?" If she says no, *don't utter a word.* End of story.

Past Injustices

There is one more grudge that daughters frequently mention when they have these cleansing sessions with Mom: past "injustices." Dissatisfied daughters seem to have a warehouse full of musty old grievances. The orthopedic shoes, the piano lessons, the ten o'clock curfew. You didn't make me go to college; you did make me go to college. You cut my hair and I wanted it long. You wouldn't buy me a kitten. You wouldn't buy me a car.

There are very few mothers who intentionally go out of their way to harm their children. Mom's good intentions usually don't count for much with a dissatisfied daughter, but they should. *Intent* is an extremely important concept in human relations, so important that criminal law is largely based upon it. Your intentions toward your daughter are not some incidental by-product of parenting, but a decades-long balancing act you do on her behalf. Day in, day out, you weigh her desires against your best instincts, the advice of the experts, the needs of the rest of the family, and so on. "I meant well," a mom will say, and her daughter will roll her eyes. Don't let your daughter trivialize all your hard work and commitment this way.

If your daughter hauls out a load of past injustices, let her take all the time she wants recounting them. Listen carefully, then offer a response like this:

> I can see that you think I've made a lot of mistakes. But what you perceive as a mistake, I thought I was doing for your good. I never deliberately did anything to hurt you. We don't have a matching perception of the past, but there is nothing we can do to change it.
>
> Whatever you may feel about my job as a parent, you have to trust me when I tell you that I did not mean you any harm. I'd really like us to wipe the slate clean. I apolo-

gize for anything I unintentionally did that hurt you, and I hope you'll forgive me.

I didn't say it would be easy! It's an act of faith to apologize to your daughter when you think her complaints are insignificant or manipulative. But look at it this way: All moms have at one time or another hurt their daughters without meaning to. If you squirm at the thought of apologizing for the curfew, mentally replace it with another injustice that you actually do regret (you need not confess that particular transgression to your daughter if she hasn't thought of it herself!). By doing this, your apology will be sincere, and your daughter will hear the sincerity in your voice.

It's a funny thing about past injustices—they really are in the eye of the beholder. One of my clients told me that for years she had felt guilty for goading her young daughter about her clumsiness. "The way I remembered it, I had teased her every day. I used to call her Bullwinkle because she'd run into all the furniture, like a bull in a china shop. Finally I told my daughter how guilty I felt. She had no idea what I was talking about, didn't remember a thing."

Just as you may regret actions your daughter didn't notice, she may feel affronted by events that barely registered on your radar. So even if her grievances seem trite, go ahead and apologize for your "errors"—it will show her that you're serious about wanting to improve the relationship. She'll remember the fact that you apologized long after she's forgotten what it was you were apologizing for.

Daughter, Here's What's Bothering Me

While your daughter is off answering the questions on your list, you should be coming up with some answers of your own. Answer every one of the questions that you asked her, and write down anything else that bothers you. Keep it simple, and use "I" statements to further the cause of measured honesty. Below are some of the comments my clients frequently make.

- I feel that I have to treat you with kid gloves.
- I sense that you are often angry with me, and I don't know why.
- I feel that you jump to conclusions about how I'll respond without giving me a chance to respond in my own way.
- I feel that you treat me disrespectfully in front of the family.
- I'm uncomfortable when you correct me in front of your children.
- I feel hurt when you criticize me.
- I feel angry when you make fun of my hobbies, friends, and activities.
- I feel taken advantage of by you.
- I feel like a repository for all your complaints, and it leaves me stressed out and frustrated.
- I never see you happy, only dissatisfied and complaining.
- I never feel really close to you. It always seems as if there's a barrier between us, a defensiveness on both our parts.

In chapter three I asked you to write a list of your daughter's attributes, and now is the ideal time to make use of that list. When you meet with your daughter, you can hand it to her before moving on to the problems. It will put her at ease, especially if there are a few humorous attributes mixed in with the serious ones.

The Showdown: You Will Do No Harm

Now that you've begun this process by giving your daughter your list of questions, don't lose momentum by waiting too long to discuss them. If you both live in the same city, schedule a follow-up meeting no more than two weeks from the day you give her your questions. If you live in different cities and won't be seeing each other in person anytime soon, set up a phone meeting.

Ask your daughter to set aside a block of time when she can speak in privacy and without interruptions. If you'll be talking over the phone, ask her to commit to an hour; if you're meeting in person, ask for two hours or more. Meet in a public place such as a restaurant or a park, so that neither of you will feel as if you are on the other's turf.

Getting hurt is what both mom and daughter are most afraid of in these meetings, so set up a few conversational safety nets at the beginning of your talk. First, assure your daughter that the purpose of the meeting is not to open up old wounds but to clear the air so you can have a happier, less stressful relationship. Repeat your vow that no matter what she tells you, you will never hold it against her, and ask her to do the same for you.

Confidentiality is a crucial element of these talks. Promise your daughter that you won't tell a soul—*including any other family member*—what you and she say to each other, and ask her to do the same. Your relationship with your daughter is between you and her, no one else. If either of you starts gossiping, you may get your perspective clouded by other people's issues.

Propose that if either of you feels too distressed to continue talking, you can stop the discussion, no questions asked. If she says she is too angry or tense to face you alone, suggest that you ask a therapist, clergyperson, or professional mediator to monitor the session so that no one gets hurt. It's better to delay the meeting for a week or so than to forge ahead onto such thin ice.

Be prepared to hear some painful news about yourself—you won't go away from this encounter unscathed. When my clients prepare for these meetings with their daughters, I tell them to envision the conversation as if it were a boxing match. You're in the ring, and you're both going to do some punching, but imagine that instead of bare fists you're wearing large, overstuffed boxing gloves filled with feathers. Written on each glove is the statement "I will do no harm." Tell your daughter, "I'm going to be as tactful as I can, and I'll be open to your criticisms. I'm going to accept what you have to say even if it hurts a bit, because I need to know how you feel."

Then, having made the boxing ring as safe as you can, hand your daughter the list of her positive attributes. When you and she have had a chuckle over it, finally ask for her responses to your questions. As you do, tell her that you have also compiled a list, which you can discuss after you've talked about her issues.

Your ultimate goals are to tell each other how you feel; resolve or put aside past grudges; and agree to begin a more honest, less defensive relationship. It sometimes takes more than one meeting to achieve this, and you probably won't achieve everything you want. If you and your daughter manage to tell each other the truth about just a few major issues, the meeting will have been a success.

Many moms and daughters run smack into the "common language" barrier as soon as they begin their session. Rina, sixty-nine, and her daughter Karen, thirty-seven, had argued for years about Rina's being, in Karen's words, "too mild." Before they had their meeting, Rina recounted this criticism to me.

"What does she mean by mild?" I asked.

"She thinks I'm old-fashioned," Rina replied without hesitation. "She thinks I'm a conservative prude."

"Have you ever asked her what mild means to her?" I queried.

"No," Rina admitted. "I tend to get defensive whenever she brings it up, and then we start arguing."

In the course of Rina's showdown with her daughter, she finally found out what Karen meant.

"She thinks I'm weak," Rina reported back to me. "It doesn't have anything to do with being prudish or old-fashioned. She thinks I don't stand up for myself to her father. She said it makes her really angry when he 'orders me around.' I had to tell her that I don't mind all that much." Rina shot me a conspiratorial glance. "Half the time I'm not even listening to him. Oh, I know that's not how she is with her husband. But I told her, 'You have your marriage, I have mine. I don't expect you to act like I do—can you do me the same favor?' "Acknowledge and accept your differences, and you and your daughter will both have more breathing room.

When you're talking with your daughter, don't jump to any conclusions about her feelings or perceptions. Don't assume you know what she has to say to you, and keep an open mind while she's speaking. Listen as you would to a person for whom English is a second language—make sure you really understand her. If she uses any words or phrases that push your buttons, ask her what she means by them.

Where Do We Go from Here?

Exposing yourself to your daughter during these meetings takes a lot of courage. Once she has told you everything she dislikes about you and you've bared your soul to her, you'll both feel raw. You need to get to a safe place, and to make that easier I've developed a few ground rules for communicating with each other from now on. They'll help you move away from your highly charged, emotionally treacherous relationship to one that is more civilized and less intense.

The process I've described here may seem overly formal, but most of these relationships are pretty stilted to begin with. The structure imposed by written questions and ground rules is actually quite helpful for moms and daughters who don't speak a common language. Besides, there is no relaxing, fun-filled way to chip through the artifice of your old relationship. As awkward as it may feel, you and your daughter must try to be honest with each other so your future visits can be relaxing and fun.

The Ground Rules

Now that we've listened to each other's complaints, let's both try to make some changes to improve our relationship. We'll both need time to adjust our behavior, so let's promise to be tolerant of each other; we're bound to make mistakes. Our new relationship will be based on mutual respect:

- We will respect each other's point of view and not assume that we know what the other is thinking or feeling.
- We will respect each other's privacy, decisions, and way of life.
- We will respect each other's feelings; we will tell the truth, but we will be tactful.
- We will respect the value of our relationship by keeping this agreement private. Neither of us will discuss it with anyone else, either friend or family member.

On to Higher Ground

Once you've had your clear-the-air session (or sessions) with your daughter, you can begin to practice what you preach. You have made the decision to deal with her honestly and treat her with respect, and you hope she will do the same. There is no guarantee about the latter. Some daughters are incapable of change, and others are perfectly comfortable with themselves and see no reason to stop complaining for your sake. Until you confront your daughter, you won't know how accommodating she'll be. But no matter what her attitude is, *you* can begin the new regime immediately. By changing the way you interact with her, you will change the relationship with or without her help—and without having to solve her problems.

Mom Power

I remember the time I actually started to cry when the phone rang.

I knew it was my daughter, and I couldn't bear to hear one more

complaint. Looking back on that moment, it was a turning point.

I realized how absurd it was to cry over a ringing phone, but I was

so frustrated with her that it all came pouring out. I had to change

things between us, or I'd be avoiding her forever.

— B a r r i e ,   a g e   f i f t y - f o u r

TAKE HEART, MOTHERS OF DISSATISFIED DAUGHTERS: From now on, instead of enduring her complaints, tantrums, and mom-bashing, you will assume power in the relationship. Most mothers tell me they feel powerless because they can't improve their daughters' lives. It's true—changing her life is beyond your control. But power does not mean controlling your daughter. Power means the ability to get what you want. You do this by changing your own behavior; that's the secret to success.

The process begins with the five most irritating things moms do, which I described in the last chapter. Reread that section carefully and stop indulging in those bad habits; it is fundamental to the other changes you'll make. By removing those annoyances from your daughter's life, you'll reduce the occasions that she lashes out at you.

In addition to refraining from irritating habits, you'll need to develop a proactive approach to your disagreeable daughter. *Proactive* means you plan your actions based on what you already know about her—it's a conscious response rather than a knee-jerk reaction. First, you'll learn how to diffuse your daughter's anger when she flares up. Second, you'll prepare a healthy defense for dealing with her criticisms and complaints. Third, you'll set a new tone for the relationship by mastering the art of light conversation and learning to organize your time together. And last but not least, you'll take control of those telephone calls. All this adds up to a new set of boundaries for the relationship—boundaries that encircle a safe, civilized, neutral territory where you and your daughter can let down your guard and have a little fun.

Extinguishing the Flare-ups: Three-Step Problem Solving

Marjorie came into my office in a terrible mood. Her daughter Sheryl was at it again, tearing into her for "interfering" with the grandkids.

"I was just being nice to them, bringing them a few little toys," Marjorie said. "Nothing expensive. A couple of puzzles." When I asked her to provide a more complete description of her daughter's outburst, the problem became clear to me.

> Sheryl had invited me to dinner, so rather than arrive empty-handed I brought the puzzles. As soon as I opened the door the kids rushed at me; they loved the puzzles and wanted to play with them right away. But instead of thanking me for giving them gifts, Sheryl got ugly. "Don't ever

bring toys into this house again!" she told me. "Why?" I asked. "You should know better," she said. Then she stomped back into the kitchen. She was mad at me for the rest of the night.

Why should a daughter resent her mother bringing gifts? Look at it from the daughter's perspective. There she is, cooking dinner, trying to get the kids settled down to eat, and feeling every inch the harried, frumpy housewife. In walks Grandma—cool, calm, collected, and bearing gifts. The kids go wild, dinner is stalled, and Mom feels even more harassed than she did before. Sheryl's ire was understandable, but as is the case with many dissatisfied daughters, she didn't immediately recognize the reasons for her own distress. She's not an even-tempered, thoughtful daughter, she's an edgy, irritable one, so she lashed out. Her mother's best bet in the future is to diffuse Sheryl's anger by helping to identify what is really bothering her. Marjorie can do this by using a simple, three-step problem-solving technique:

1. State the problem.
2. State your feelings.
3. Ask for what you want: an explanation, a resolution, or a compromise.

Now, don't expect your irritable daughter to greet your questions with a welcoming smile. Her attitude does not matter; yours does. Stay calm and listen to the information she gives you, regardless of her tone of voice. In the unwanted gift scenario, the conversation might go like this:

MOTHER: I get the impression you're very angry with me.
DAUGHTER: Brilliant deduction, Mom.
MOTHER: I'm confused. I don't understand why you're angry.
DAUGHTER: You know damn well why I'm angry.

MOTHER: No, honey, I really don't. I'd like you to explain why you're angry and why you don't like me to bring the kids gifts.

DAUGHTER: Okay, I'll spell it out for you. The kids were all ready to eat and you waltz in here like the Queen of Sheba with presents and get them all riled up. Every time they see you they get a toy. I don't give them presents all the time, so what does that make me? I'm sick of it!

You have now received the information you needed: Your daughter wants to maintain control over the dinner hour, and she feels uncomfortable about you lavishing gifts on her children. You have two choices. You can argue with her ("They're my grandkids. Why can't I bring them a present?") or you can think about what she has told you. I recommend the latter. Simply say to your daughter, "I'll think about that," and walk into the other room, leaving her alone to simmer down. If her request is basically reasonable—*whether or not you like it*—respect her wishes from now on. If it seems outlandish, suggest a compromise or alternate solution.

The same rules apply to situations where your daughter is being thoughtless or hurtful. I've found that often the daughter doesn't even realize she's offending Mom, yet Mom assumes the daughter is purposely insulting her. It goes back to expecting your daughter to intuit your innermost feelings. "If she really loved me, she'd do what I want without my having to ask," moms will insist. But our daughters are not mind readers; it has nothing to do with their love for us.

Nancy, seventy-one, had begun to dread family get-togethers because her three daughters would always end up telling humorous "Mom" stories. They thought it was all in good-natured fun, but Nancy felt as if they were mocking her.

Nancy used the three-step method to solve what she considered a mom-bashing trend with her daughters. She pulled aside each daughter separately and stated the problem: "I want to talk to you about the way you make fun of me." Then she explained how she felt: "I feel humiliated when you do that, and it makes me very uncomfortable." Finally, she suggested a solution: "Please, I'd appreciate it if in the future you'd stop telling humorous stories about me." Her daughters were surprised by Nancy's "sensitivity," but they apologized and stopped the behavior.

An important element of this strategy is to use "I" messages, not "you" messages, when speaking to your daughter. "I" messages are a tried-and-true therapists' tool, and they are remarkably effective. The concept is simple: If you begin a sentence with the word *you,* your statement will usually sound like an accusation. For example: "You're always late to pick me up." If you begin your sentence with the word *I,* you force yourself to think about your part in the equation. You take responsibility for your feelings, rather than just pointing a finger at the wrongdoer. In return, your listener is apt to be more receptive. Combined with the three-step problem-solving process, the previous statement becomes less harsh: "I get upset when we have plans and you're not on time to pick me up. I feel neglected when that happens. I would prefer a looser time frame—say half an hour—and rather than have me wait in front of my building at a specific time, you can buzz me down when you arrive."

By taking this approach, you are no longer the passive victim of your daughter's schedule, nor are you an impotent complainer. You have stated the problem, told her how you feel about it, and suggested a solution, all the while taking responsibility for your role in the situation. You have assumed a position of power.

Whenever your dissatisfied daughter flares up at you or behaves thoughtlessly, use the three-step method to diffuse her anger and get to a reasonable solution. In time, you'll pinpoint many of the things you and your daughter do to push each other's buttons. Once you eliminate those from your relationship, the tension will begin to fade.

Preparing a Healthy Defense

Mothers usually rely on a combination of lying and defensiveness to get through a conversation with a dissatisfied daughter. They lie about their true feelings, and they defend against their daughters' criticisms. The constant feinting and ducking leaves Mom angry, drained, and ever more anxious about the next encounter with daughter dearest.

In order to ratchet down your anxiety level, you must plan your responses to your daughter well in advance of your conversations with her. I call this "preparing a healthy defense" because it's different than the lying and defending that mothers typically resort to. By preparing a healthy defense, you stay in control of the conversation.

If you've followed my advice, you no longer hound your daughter with questions. However, she may still hound you with complaints, criticisms, and hard-luck tales, and that's where moms tend to falter and resort to the old conversational techniques. Instead, whenever you speak to your daughter remember your new philosophy:

- My daughter and I are separate individuals.
- Her problems are hers, not mine, and I cannot solve them for her.
- I deserve to be treated with respect, and I will not tolerate mom-bashing.

By recognizing that you and your daughter are separate individuals and you can't solve her problems, you instantly relieve yourself of having to come up with solutions for her. As I noted in chapter seven, most of the time she doesn't want solutions anyway; complaining is your daughter's way of eliciting sympathy (love) from you.

How do you respond to her grousing if you're not going to

solve her problems? By employing a little harmless commiseration—that is, lip service. Act sympathetic, even if you don't feel terribly sorry for her. Validate her feelings of frustration and unhappiness, rather than trying to counter them with cheery comments such as "Come on, honey, a flat tire isn't the end of the world." Instead, be supportive: "That's awful. What a shame." You need do nothing more than sympathize with her plight, and in most cases you'll be giving her the emotional response she needs.

If it rankles you to "encourage" her negative outlook on life, remember that her emotional needs and personality are well established once she's an adult. Arguing with her about whether or not a flat tire is a disaster *will not change her outlook*. You don't have the power to change her by arguing with her. So give her what she needs—sympathy, love, and her daily fix of Mom's soothing voice.

Some daughters insist that Mom become fully involved in the drama of their dilemma, pleading, "What should I do, Mom?" and then (usually) ignoring Mom's suggestions. If she hasn't heeded your advice in the past, don't offer it anymore. Gently tell her, "I'm at a loss. I really can't help you with your problem. You'll just have to work out some answers on your own. I trust in you."

Countering Her Attacks

A more difficult challenge is dealing with your daughter's criticism and mom-bashing. One of the reasons moms put up with rude, disrespectful daughters is that they fear abandonment. A dissatisfied daughter might think nothing of telling Mom, "I'm never speaking to you again!" at very little provocation. You must understand that in most cases, she does not mean it. To plan an effective defense when dealing with an unpleasant daughter, you can't always be afraid of her. You must be prepared for her displeasure, and confident enough to know that even if she stalks off, she's not gone for good.

Besides, would it be so terrible to have her out of your life for a little while? "Give her some time to miss you," I urge my clients. Sometimes it takes a month, sometimes six; in rare cases it may even take a year or two. But eventually, nearly all dissatisfied daughters come back to Mom's door. If your daughter has been calling you daily or weekly all her life, she needs you. No matter how off-kilter the relationship may feel, that level of contact is an important indicator of the bond between you.

You must either resolve not to put up with mom-bashing or resign yourself to being a doormat for the rest of your life. When your daughter begins to criticize or belittle you, remember these cardinal rules:

Never explain or defend your daughter's bad behavior. Don't let her off the hook by making apologies for her if you're among other people. If it's just you and she, don't make internal excuses for her—tell her outright that you don't like the way she's acting.

Never explain or defend your own behavior. If your daughter starts hectoring you about your "obsession" with bridge, use measured honesty and tell her, "I do like playing bridge, and I'm not going to apologize for it. I'm darn good!" Stick to your guns, and leaven your statements with humor whenever you can. If she won't let up, toss the ball back in her court: "I don't have a problem with your obsession with your aerobics class. Each to her own—let's call it a draw."

If you don't like what she's doing, leave the room or hang up the phone. You can and should be a lady about it, but the moment your daughter starts crossing the line into rudeness, say, "I really can't talk anymore. I'll talk to you another time. Goodbye." and hang up. Don't slam down the receiver; always try to keep your end of the relationship civil. If you're sitting at the dinner table and your daughter starts mom-bashing you, rise from your chair and say, "I'm feeling very uncomfortable with the way this conversation is going. Let's change the subject or I'm going to make my exit." If your daughter won't comply, leave the room. You don't have to make a big scene out of it or limp off like a wounded dog; you are aiming for a dignified, graceful exit. Dignity commands respect. There will be other dinners; meanwhile, you must stand up for yourself.

Acknowledge the truth. Moms will often sidestep the truth because acknowledging it might lead to an argument. From now on, if your daughter misbehaves, tell it like you see it. If she accuses you of disapproving of her, don't argue. Agree with truthful statements.

Doris, sixty, first put this policy into practice when her dissatisfied daughter threatened to spoil another daughter's birthday celebration:

> I took Candace and Joan to lunch for Joan's birthday. As usual, Candace dominated the conversation with her complaints: the restaurant was cold, the waitress was inattentive, the food was lousy. Finally I told her to quiet down; she was ruining Joan's birthday. Candace sulked in silence for the rest of the meal, but at least Joan and I got to enjoy ourselves.
>
> Later Candace accused me of being critical. "Yes, I am," I said. "Your behavior was unacceptable." "I don't like you telling me off in public," she said. "I didn't think you would," I answered. Then I ended the conversation. I felt vindicated.

It's all about setting a standard of civilized behavior for yourself and your daughter and enforcing that standard. Deep down, your daughter probably wonders why you've put up with her nonsense all these years anyway. After all, she's not mentally ill, she's just a sourpuss. Respect her enough to insist that she behave civilly.

Once you get past the complaints and have effectively countered your daughter's put-downs, you'll be able to move on to the next level: a casual, friendly, mother-daughter conversation.

Salvation in the Superficial: The Art of Light Conversation

Anyone who watches TV knows that conversations between mother and daughter are supposed to be *meaningful*. On television, moms and daughters share intimacies, reveal heartbreaking secrets, cry, hug, storm out of the room, and race back in again declaring eternal love. That's what it takes to keep an audience's interest.

In real life, striving for meaning in every conversation puts a damper on a relationship. Intimate, soul-searching discussions are exhausting. They are not always pleasant and can leave both sides feeling overexposed. But because of the way conversations are portrayed in movies and on TV, many of us assume that unless our daughters tell us exactly what they are feeling about the important issues in their lives, we aren't really talking. So we interrogate them, they flare up, and we end up bickering instead of conversing.

One of the mothers I counsel revealed to me that after each of our hour-long private sessions, she went home and took a two-hour nap. "It really wears me out," she confessed. Thinking so intently about your feelings, motives, and future plans is hard work. My clients willingly sign on for this level of self-examination; your daughter did not. If you demand it from her every time you speak to her, she's going to respond by recounting her litany of hardships, sniping at you, or hanging up on you.

The moms I counsel are astonished when I tell them that when conversing with their daughters, the breakdown should be 5 percent intimate conversation, 95 percent casual chit chat. It's no sin if the conversation is entirely superficial. Mothers are quite unnerved by this notion, so accustomed are they to poking around in their daughters' personal lives or regaling them with their own intimate problems. After a few moments of silence, a mother will usually ask, "But what are we going to talk about?"

My answer to that is, "What would you talk about with a friend?" You discuss the latest news story, TV shows, movies. You tell her about books you've read, how the vegetable garden is doing, the quirky habits of your new hairdresser. You describe the great vacation spot you read about in a travel magazine, the kids you read to at the library, the new restaurant you've discovered. In short, you develop the art of light conversation.

There *is* an art to it, and you may already excel. Think about the discussions you have with your friends. Most would have little patience with you if you continually nagged them for personal information or insisted on only discussing family matters. With your daughter, too, you must put some effort into making your conversations interesting. In chapter three I suggested that you try to develop interests in common with your daughter. If you do that, you'll automatically have a subject to discuss, be it needlepoint, neighborhood politics, or rose gardening.

Imagine the cumulative effect of, say, two months' worth of nonintrusive, light conversation with your daughter. At first she may greet your new approach with suspicion or even derision ("Since when do you care about politics!"), but take it in stride and stick to your plan. After several weeks, she'll begin to realize that conversations with you can be easygoing, interesting, and pleasant. (Of course, if you are a Republican and your daughter is a Democrat, don't discuss politics. Stay on neutral territory.)

The other benefit to developing light conversation is that it gives you something to say as you deflect your daughter's complaints. Fanny, a gregarious mom in her early seventies, recounted her first attempts at light conversation with her malcontent daughter, Barbara:

Barb's main occupation in life is complaining about her health. I decided that from now on, I'd allow her five minutes of health complaints, and then I'd switch the subject. It was like trying to pull a horse away from the feeding trough.

I made sympathetic noises for the first five minutes, with a few comments like "I'm sure the doctor will want to hear about that." Then I said, "Did you see that new cooking show about Mexican food?"

"Mom," she said, "you know Mexican food gives me indigestion."

"They were making this dish called mole," I told her. "It's with chicken and a delicious dark sauce made with chocolate."

"I told you, it makes me sick," she whined.

"Chocolate, Barb. It has chocolate."

"Chicken with chocolate?" she finally asked. Aha! I had her! We talked about the chocolate sauce for a few minutes and then I got off the phone, quick. I felt like I should do victory laps around the Olympic Stadium.

There truly is salvation in the superficial. Light conversation is diverting, playful, and most of all, nonthreatening. You will not be missing out on anything important in your daughter's life by focusing on fun topics rather than "big issues" or the details of her daily existence. As you become more accustomed to chatting with her as if she were a friend, you may discover that you and she have more in common than you thought. Maybe you both have a secret desire to learn piano, or a love of the same author.

Consider these light conversations to be fresh soil that you're spreading over the field that was once spiked with land mines. Light conversation is safe territory. When your daughter feels safe, she'll be less likely to lash out at you. When she stops lashing out, you'll feel safer, too.

Organized Time: Field Trips and Projects

Much of our interaction with our daughters takes place over the phone, where it's relatively easy to control the conversation (I'll share my favorite telephone techniques a little later in this chapter). Face-to-face visits are a whole different animal.

It's typical for moms and daughters to get into a routine, like the Thursday night dinners described by Leslie in chapter seven. Often both women have grown to dread this prescribed time together. As one of my clients put it, "After we get through talking about her kids, taking apart her husband, and complaining about what her girlfriend didn't do, it's just her and me. There's not much to say, so we start recycling the complaints. By the end of dinner I can't wait to get away from her."

Your daughter is not likely to change this scenario, even if she, too, is weary of it. You are the one who'll have to take the lead in turning your coffee klatch into organized time—either field trips or household projects. Now that you're not going to spend more than 5 percent of your time on gut-level discussions, you don't have to sit there gazing at each other across the kitchen table. You can take a walk, take a drive, get your nails done together. Even errands can be fun when there are two of you dipping in and out of this store and that, cruising through the weekend chores. Your daughter will appreciate being able to kill two birds with one stone, and one of you will be there to wait in the car if parking spaces are scant. You'll be doing her a favor, and you can get some of your own errands done, too.

It makes no difference whether you organize the visit beforehand or suggest a spur-of-the-moment activity, as long as you take action. Here are a few of the field trips my clients have enjoyed.

- Drive to a part of town you don't usually visit, and look at the homes and architecture.

- Take a bicycle ride—bikes can be rented at many public parks and beaches.
- Check your local paper for free events such as seasonal craft fairs or music festivals.
- Play tourist for a day; board a tour bus and learn some of your home town's history.
- Join a quilting group together or take a cooking class.
- Take the kids to the park, the zoo, the local fire station, the library.
- Go to a movie, play, or the museum.
- Go antiquing.

Train yourself to be imaginative, and don't overlook places near your home that have become part of the background scenery to you. A stroll to the park to watch the local dog-training class in action can be tremendously enjoyable. Your goal is to find activities that take the focus off the personal and give you and your daughter something new to laugh about or discuss.

If you don't feel like planning an outing every time you see your daughter or if time is an issue, tackle a project at her house or yours. Hem all the raggedy sheets and pillowcases; line the kitchen shelves and drawers; organize the Christmas decorations. Women's magazines are full of suggestions for household projects. One mother I know, an admitted clean freak, turned her near obsession to good use on her visits with her daughter:

> We got into a pattern over the summer. One week we'd wash her two dogs—take them out in the back yard with a big metal tub, lather them up, hose them off, then try to "groom" them with brushes and bows. We'd get hysterical trying to make those mutts beautiful.
>
> On weeks when we didn't wash the dogs, we'd wash and wax our cars. It took a couple of hours and we'd be dead tired afterward, but it was surprisingly pleasant. We were working too hard to fight.

Some of my own fondest memories are of working side by side with my mother at my parents' dairy farm in Winterport, Maine. My mother and father purchased the farm when I was eighteen and, turning their backs on city life forever, dove into a rural existence. I never lived on the farm with them, but I'd visit for a month every summer. Don't think my mother and I just sat there smiling at each other—she put me to work. We'd sew together, bake together, prepare vegetables for canning. We'd weed and fertilize the garden. The days were busy, but very satisfying. Sometimes she and I hardly spoke except to discuss that day's project, although we did sing a lot of songs together and sip a little sherry now and then. No stress, no interrogation, no "So what are you going to do with your life?" Just living, day to day.

Take your visits with your daughter one day at a time, and try to make those visits as uncomplicated and enjoyable as possible. If a little voice inside you complains, "Why do I have to be the one to think up all the activities?" ignore it. By taking the initiative, you'll gain the power you desire in your relationship. Eventually your daughter might catch on and start planning some field trips or projects of her own.

Escaping the Tyranny of the Telephone, or Twenty Minutes Is Enough for God and Anyone

The phone rings. Your stomach knots. You glance anxiously at the clock and do lightening-fast calculations: Could it be your daughter? What were her most recent crises and complaints? Do you have an hour to spare? Should you just let it ring? But what if it's someone else?

The telephone has been referred to as an umbilical cord between mother and daughter. If your daughter is a chronic complainer, the cord can feel more like a leash—or a noose. I've counseled moms whose daughters call them two, three, even four times a day to report their latest travails. Even if you master all the communication skills I've described in this chapter, you'll find that the telephone demands special tactics.

First you must decide how often you want to talk to your daughter, what time is convenient for you, and how long you want the conversation to last. You may recall my theory that many daughters like to touch base at least once a day for mom's nurturance. I feel that once a day is fair, so long as your daughter is not verbally abusing you. If the calls are abusive, you ought not to put up with them, period. Your daughter, or you and she together, should get professional help in any cases of abusive behavior. For all other daughters, one twenty-minute phone call a day should suffice.

The trick, of course, is implementing the one-call, twenty-minute rule. You might introduce the concept to your daughter this way: "You know, I love it that you like to chat every day. But from now on I've decided to limit the time I spend on the phone with family and friends, because I seem to be chatting my life away. So if I end a conversation earlier than I used to do, that's why. And I'll probably only be able to talk once a day."

In case your daughter doesn't quite grasp your intent, you'll need to have a phone-taming strategy in place. You want to limit the number of calls; make sure you talk when it's convenient for you; and limit the duration of the call to twenty minutes.

1. *Limit the number of calls.* This basically amounts to not answering all of her calls. If you don't already have an answering machine or service, get one. The services offered through the phone company are easy to use—perfect for moms who are uncomfortable with high-tech answering machines. Answering machines, on the other hand, give you the lovely option of "screening" your calls, that is, listening in while the caller leaves a message.

Many phone companies also offer a "selective ring" service, which assigns a unique ring to your daughter's number so that you instantly know if it's she on the other end. And there are other caller-ID tools available as well, through mail-order catalogs or at your local electronics store.

There is always the option of letting the phone ring without finding out who called. For most women this is pure torture, but if you're made of strong enough stuff, more power to you!

2. *Talk at your convenience.* Some mothers and daughters are able to agree on a time to check in each day. If your schedule is too complicated for that, you have several options. You can call her—a preemptive strike will ensure that you talk when you want to. Or you can wait until she calls at a convenient time to answer the phone. Or, if you're too pressed for time to talk but want to check in, you can call her when you know she'll be out and leave a message on her machine.

3. *Limit the call to twenty minutes.* The best method for this, and the one that I use, is to get a loud timer and keep it near the phone, so that the person on the other end will be able to hear when it goes off. When your daughter calls, set the timer for twenty minutes. Then—*BING*—"Oops! I have to

- turn off the sprinklers
- take something out of the oven
- help Dad with the car
- get to the post office
- get ready for my lunch date
- take the dog for his walk

. . . so we'll catch up tomorrow. Bye, sweetie."

To Accept Is Divine

I have seen scores of mothers achieve tremendous changes in their relationships with their dissatisfied daughters by using the methods described in these pages. Once you've eliminated the land mines, developed a way to communicate honestly with your daughter, and set up some new boundaries, your life will improve. But there is one more thing you must do in order to be at peace with yourself and your daughter: You must accept her for who she is. She may never be the world's most entertaining and devoted companion, and she may never reach the potential you once hoped she would. Try to let go of your old expectations and behold your real-life daughter—she is yours and you are hers. Accept her lovingly, and in time she will accept you too.

PART FOUR

THE DISTANT DAUGHTER

Missing Daughters

My daughter and I only see each other twice a year. Ever since her
father died, she seems to want nothing to do with me. When she
visits she acts happy enough, but then she leaves and I don't hear
from her for months. No calls, no cards. She doesn't answer my
letters. I wish she would tell me what's wrong. I can only fix it if I
know what's broken.

— *C h a r l o t t e ,   a g e   s e v e n t y - s i x*

WHEN A DAUGHTER WITHDRAWS FROM HER FAMILY, THE
effect is catastrophic. It's as if she's detonated a bomb in the midst
of the living room—there's a hole in everyone's life that doesn't
close up until the daughter is ready to come back again. Meanwhile, the loss is overwhelming.

It frequently takes years for a mother to realize that her daughter has purposely chosen to distance herself. After two or three
years of dwindling phone calls and visits, Mom will begin to get
an inkling that something traumatic is shifting in her relationship
with her daughter. But often it's not until six or seven years of
decreasing contact that a mother finally admits to herself, "My
daughter does not want to see me anymore." Then, when the

daughter's intent has become undeniable, Mom will slowly sink into mourning.

Mothers of distant daughters are heartbroken, numb, guilt-ridden, and lonely. They come to me seeking solace, but I'm usually able to offer more: the very reasonable expectation that their daughter will someday return. In the great majority of cases, the distant daughter does eventually reconcile with her parents. Her change of heart is often set off by a life event such as a death, birth, or the serious illness of a relative, but sometimes it's just a matter of enough time having passed. The daughter may see a film, read a book, attend a wedding, or see a news story on TV that suddenly makes her long to reconnect with her mother and family.

My work with mothers of distant daughters is twofold. First, I help them understand the part they may have played in their daughters' withdrawal. Then I teach them how to change their behavior, adjust their expectations, and reach out to their daughters again and again, until all options are exhausted. Even if your daughter has been gone for years and you've resigned yourself to never seeing her again, that doesn't mean she won't someday knock on your door.

This chapter is devoted to the first part of the process: understanding why your daughter withdrew and what your role might have been. I'll share with you some of the most common circumstances that drive daughters away from the family (although there are countless reasons why daughters leave, certain themes seem to crop up repeatedly), and I'll explain how a daughter's absence affects her mother's marriage, friendships, and sense of well-being for years after the separation. It's important to hear these war stories so that you'll be able to put your pain in some kind of context. Many mothers never tell a soul outside of the family that their daughter is missing; they bear their loss in silence. The family itself may not offer much consolation, since members usually blame one another for the daughter's departure. Mom blames Dad, Dad blames Mom, the siblings blame one another and Mom and Dad. It's a sad fact that a tragedy such as this usually drives families apart just when they need each other the most.

To leave one's mother, to break that bond, takes a tremendous amount of strength. Your daughter's pain must run very deep for her to have chosen this path. To win her back, you must be prepared to hear her side of the story, to let down your defenses and open your heart to her. You must be willing to forgive her and to ask for her forgiveness. This process, which I will describe in chapter eleven, can be extremely difficult for both mother and daughter, but I've seen so many success stories that I feel confident in urging you to try it. You have nothing more to lose, and everything to gain.

You Can't Control a Missing Person

Blameless and bewildered. That's how many mothers of distant daughters first present themselves to me. "We had a perfectly normal, happy home," a mom will insist. "I have no idea why my daughter has abandoned us." In some instances this is true, but in at least half of the cases I see, the mom and daughter are equally to blame for the rift between them. These situations inevitably involve a mother who tries to control her daughter and a daughter who is unwilling or unable to deal with her overbearing mom. These daughters choose flight over fight. Instead of combating Mom to assert their independence, they simply remove themselves from her orbit.

The more a controlling mother tries to force herself into her distant daughter's life, the more the daughter will withdraw. Sadly, the mothers are usually blind to their own flaws. It's not uncommon for such a mom to be in counseling for six months before admitting that, well, maybe she was a little heavy-handed with her daughter. True, she had been known to toss the contents of her adolescent daughter's closet in the Dumpster because she didn't approve of the mess. And yes, she was very particular and outspoken about her daughter's friends, the way she cut her hair, who she dated, where she shopped, what she wore. . . .

It's difficult for these mothers to understand that their intense concern for their daughters may have been inappropriate, even when the daughters were teenagers. What a mom may pooh-pooh as typical mother shenanigans, her daughter may have experienced as unbearable oppression. It all depends on the daughter and mother. Even within a single family, one daughter may be able to shrug off Mom's advice and intrusiveness, while another daughter finds it intolerable. One daughter may deal with Mom by charming her, another by rebelling. When these daughters reach adulthood, the pattern continues. The charmer goes on sweet-talking Mom; the rebel distances herself. But Mom cannot continue to treat these women as she did when they were girls, or her distant daughter may drift away permanently.

Your Daughter Didn't Fail, the Fantasy Failed

In an effort to speed things along with moms who are reluctant to acknowledge their domineering tendencies, I ask them what their expectations were for their daughters. I've discovered that many controlling moms have invented an extravagant fairy tale about how life should be with their grown daughter. When an extremely strong mother harbors outrageous expectations, it isn't unusual for her daughter to distance herself as a matter of survival. In these cases, Mom has to carefully list every one of her expectations (as I asked you to do in chapter three), acknowledge which of them are unrealistic, and let those go.

All moms indulge in fairy tales about their daughters, and many are perfectly harmless. I had a fairy tale myself. Before my first grandchild was born (I now have eight of them), I used to picture my daughter and me strolling with the baby buggy to the corner ice-cream store. We'd happily lick our vanilla cones as neighbors stopped to coo and marvel over our little angel. Then we'd go shopping together—my daughter would want to spend all her free time shopping with me—and finally we'd stroll home as the sun set over the neighborhood.

The ice-cream fantasy did happen—once. The restaurant was loud and crowded with strangers. The ice cream was messy and dripped all over the place. A man a few tables away stared at my diamond ring while we ate, and when we left the restaurant he followed us out. As we ducked into a side street to hide from him, I thought to myself, "This is my fantasy? This is what I've been waiting for all these years? What a letdown!"

My fairy tale was a frivolous one that was easy to let go of, but many moms are loath to give up their daughter fantasies. Interestingly, these dreams often have little to do with how successful or fulfilled the daughter herself will be. Instead, the fantasies are all about how the grown daughter will behave toward Mom. As Rose, sixty-three, recounted her longtime fantasies about her daughter, her tone shifted between irony and wistfulness:

> I can tell you exactly what I used to fantasize. We'd go
> shopping together, and I'd help her pick out her clothes.
> We'd get our hair done together. She'd have girlfriends,
> sure, but none whom she could tell her secrets to the way
> she could to me. When she got married, boy, would I make
> her a wedding! And when she had kids, they'd think of me
> as their "other mommy." My house would be a second
> home to them; we'd all be one big happy family.

Actually, this is just the sort of ultraclose relationship many mothers *claim* to have with their daughter. Mothers of dependent daughters are especially prone to bragging that they and their girl are "best friends." Between the mothers who exaggerate their closeness to their daughters and those whose daughters are dependent, it can seem as if everyone but you is sipping cider cheek to cheek with her grown daughter each afternoon. I can assure you that this is not the case.

Many controlling mothers become victims of their own unrealistic expectations and the bragging of other moms. It's a combination that makes both mother and daughter miserable. Whatever bond Mom has with her own daughter, it seems less than what Mrs. Jones down the street has with *hers*. The overbearing mother doggedly tries to "fix" her relationship by announcing her dissatisfaction to her daughter, insisting on more contact, swamping her with newspaper clippings and phone calls, and constantly comparing the daughter's level of devotion to that of all those other, better daughters. In response, the distant daughter pulls further and further away from her mother.

Although it can be very difficult for a controlling mother to accept partial responsibility for her daughter's abandonment, that is the first step toward healing. Her advantage is that if she can change her behavior and prove that she is sincere about the change, she can (usually) woo her daughter back again. The other mothers I counsel are embroiled in circumstances that are more complex than a personality clash or struggle of wills. Although the following list is by no means comprehensive, distant-daughter cases often fall into one of these categories:

- The daughter feels betrayed or abused by events that happened years earlier
- The daughter marries someone who does not get along with the parents or of whom the parents disapprove
- The daughter is vying with her mother for her father's love
- The daughter blames Mom and sides with Dad in a divorce
- The daughter hates Mom's new husband
- The daughter is battling Mom over money
- The daughter withdraws as her mother gets older and needier
- The daughter is ashamed of her parents due to a clash of values or culture

I'm going to briefly discuss each of these situations in the hopes that you'll be able to identify with one or several of them. The circumstances often overlap: Daughter is a Daddy's girl and has always vied for his attention; then he and Mom get divorced and the daughter sides with Dad; then Mom gets remarried and the daughter hates the new husband. Unfortunately, I've seen countless variations on this theme. But as our daughters get older and experience life's vagaries for themselves, they sometimes begin to see why we moms made the decisions we did. That's why it pays to hang in there; time can be a mother's greatest ally.

Betrayals, Real and Imagined

Some daughters distance themselves from their mothers or parents as punishment for a betrayal or abuse they claim occurred during their youth. Certainly some mothers are abusive, and as I've said earlier, the suggestions in this book won't help them. But there are many other moms who tried their best to raise a family—often in difficult circumstances—only to have a daughter angrily announce that her childhood was abysmal and she has no more use for her parents.

The parental betrayals I've listened to include moving to another city, insisting that a daughter go to a specific university, divorce and/or remarriage, loss of financial stability and social status, getting rid of a beloved pet, being too strict, encouraging a pregnant teenager to get an abortion, and many more. In some of these cases the mother deeply regretted her actions. In other instances the daughter's claims of abuse or betrayal were flatly denied by her mother, leading to an endless round of "You did," "I did not."

When Merrill, thirty-one, entered my office I had to keep myself from staring: she weighed at least two hundred and fifty pounds. As she eased herself down on my sofa, she told me that she was here to talk about her mother, Arlene. According to Merrill, her mother had beaten her and made family life wretched.

> To this day I can't sit down to a meal without being flooded with awful memories, because every meal in our house was such a disaster. I only talk to my mother a couple of times a year because I'd prefer to just put my past behind me. Now she says she wants to be friends again, to try and make up for lost time. I told her, "I can't deal with you alone."

This was a wise decision on Merrill's part, because it's often impossible for estranged mothers and daughters to reconnect without a professional mediator to help them discuss their pent-up anger and resentments.

Merrill, Arlene, and I embarked on a series of sessions that lasted about a year. Arlene, while somewhat reserved, seemed to genuinely desire a closer relationship with her daughter. But she and Merrill disagreed fiercely about the extent of the beatings Merrill claimed to have received as a child. Merrill recalled weekly spankings or lashings with a belt; Arlene vehemently denied it and said she flew off the handle two or three times a year, and only twice had she resorted to a belt. There was no way for me to discern the truth; meanwhile, week after week, Merrill told her mother, "I want you to listen to everything I have to say about my childhood."

"You've made it clear," Arlene would reply. "What do you want me to do?"

"I want you to suffer."

"I have suffered. I am suffering," Arlene would say.

"I want you to apologize."

"I am very, very sorry for anything I've done to make you unhappy."

"Well, that doesn't really help. You can't take away my past," Merrill would insist.

"I never promised you I'd be Mary Poppins," Arlene would finally blurt out in frustration. "What is it that you want from me? I just can't please you."

It may not ever be possible for a betrayed daughter and her mother to agree on a single version of the past. But they can agree to disagree, and move on to a new, different relationship. I try to help these women establish the same kind of neutral territory I described in the chapters about dissatisfied daughters. Perhaps their relationship will be more superficial than the mother would like, but at least they'll be talking to each other. Neither mother nor daughter has to be right or wrong to find this common ground. All they need is the mutual desire to get back on speaking terms.

My Husband or My Mother

The conflict between mothers-in-law and husbands is an ancient one. In *The Golden Bough,* Sir James George Frazer comments that "the awe and dread with which the untutored savage contemplates his mother-in-law are amongst the most familiar facts of anthropology." Modern mothers-in-law often seem to inspire equal trepidation in today's husbands. At one time marrying outside your clan was the big taboo; nowadays "mixed marriages" are commonplace, but even if parents are tolerant in that arena, there are many other reasons they may reject a daughter's husband: he doesn't make enough money, he's not ambitious enough, he's divorced, he's too slick, he doesn't have a college degree—he's just not good enough for her.

Although parents' objections are sometimes prejudiced or snobbish, in many instances they have good reason to worry. Young women do make foolish choices, and it's excruciating to watch your daughter fall in love with a man who is clearly a bad seed. Visions of her divorce, troubled kids, custody battles, and financial doom dance before your eyes day and night. You only have a brief window of opportunity—before they're married—to warn her away from disaster. If that doesn't work and she weds him anyhow, you've already set the stage for an acrimonious relationship with your son-in-law. That places your daughter in the middle of a tug-of-war between her mother and her husband. If she can't take the stress, she may choose to distance herself from you. Very likely her husband will urge her to do just that. If they move to another city or state—or country—you run the risk of gradually losing contact with her. It naturally follows that you won't be allowed much access to her children, either.

Once the deed is done and your daughter has married Mr. Wrong, the prudent move is to accept the situation and immediately make peace with the couple so you can stay in contact with them. Few of us, however, are that self-possessed. In most cases a barely concealed dislike smolders between the husband and the in-laws, causing the daughter much distress. The only way to avoid the tension is to avoid her mother and father, and that is the beginning of the distancing process. Unless a mother is able to put her daughter at ease about her husband, the distance will only increase over the years.

As a mother, you must ask yourself which is most important: pointing out your son-in-law's deficiencies to your daughter, or staying on good terms with her. Unless he is abusing her or she seems very unhappy, there's no reason for the two of you to discuss him. You don't have to like him; you just have to accept her choice. You can bridge the rift between you and your daughter by reframing your relationship with her so that it doesn't threaten him. Convince her that the time you spend together will be enjoyable, not stressful, and you can win back your daughter's affection and companionship.

My Heart Belongs to Daddy

Daddy dressed her up and took her to the movies as soon as she could stay awake long enough. Daddy took her with him to visit friends and stop for ice cream. He whispered to her that one day he would take her to Mexico and leave me and her brother behind. He was nurturing and protective of her, and he made her feel very special. But she always viewed me as a rival for her father's affection, and because of that we were never close. My daughter became my competition.

Olga, sixty-five, had come to my office after a brief cancer scare. A lump in her breast had turned out to be benign, but that brush with illness left her determined to patch up some of the holes in her life, particularly with her estranged daughter, Jillian. Theirs was a story I have heard quite often—Jillian was a Daddy's girl who had never felt close to her mother. Freud termed this the Electra complex, and it is at the root of many distant-daughter problems.

It typically begins, as in Olga's case, with a father who dotes on his daughter. Often the little girl is the family's only daughter, or the firstborn, or the baby. Dad and his daughter form a special bond, and the daughter views Mom as a rival for Dad's time and love. Very often, the father and daughter start to collude against Mom when the girl is still quite young. It begins, as Olga testified, with whispered asides: *Mom doesn't get it. She's no fun. Finish your chores and I'll take you to the mall, just you and me.* The unspoken message is that Mom is outside the golden circle—Dad and daughter share the same tastes, opinions, and lust for life, while boring old Mom is only interested in hearth and home.

Revisit the scene in twenty years, and you'll frequently find the same dynamic. Mom will prepare a Thanksgiving dinner, and from the moment Daughter walks in the front door, the collusion begins:

"She's using the old china? Dad! Don't we have Grandma's good china?"

"You know your mother. . . ."

"What's wrong with her, Dad? Did she manage not to burn the potatoes this time?"

"Let's hope for the best, honey."

And so on. The mom-bashing can be subtle or overt, can come across as harmless teasing or intentional cruelty.

When does the relationship between mother and daughter turn from dissatisfied to distant? As soon as Mom refuses to take it anymore. Typically the crisis occurs after mother or daughter has gone to a therapist or joined some sort of support group. In the therapist's office, the Electra complex quickly rises up in all its glory, like the Statue of Liberty thrusting out of New York harbor. Once it is out in the open, the daughter's disapproval of and rivalry with Mom can be seen for what it is: intrusive, inappropriate behavior; a thorn in her parents' marriage. The decades-old collusion between Dad and his daughter is brought into the light, and Dad has to take a stand. When put on the spot, he will usually take his place alongside Mom. After all, he probably never intended his relationship with his daughter to threaten his marriage; he loves his wife. The day Mom and Dad stand together and say, "Enough! From now on you'll treat your mother with respect," is an earth-shattering day for the daughter. It is very common for a daughter to distance herself from her family after this sort of confrontation.

In cases such as this, a period of distance can actually be a good thing, because the daughter will need time to reevaluate her relationship with both her parents. If she's in therapy, so much the better; her therapist can help her adjust to life as a real woman as opposed to Daddy's special pet (Daddy's girls often have a host of problems relating to men, which I won't go into here). When Mom is ready for a reconciliation, she can use the techniques in the next chapter to approach her distant daughter as an equal and a potential friend. These cases often have happy endings, especially as the daughter grows older and becomes a mom herself.

A similar but sadder scenario can come about when a father is cold and aloof to his daughter. In these cases the daughter wishes she could be a daddy's girl, but Dad wants nothing to do with her. Deprived of her father's affection, the young girl will often become rebellious or depressed; she'll try anything to grab his attention. Meanwhile Mom—the lucky recipient of Dad's love—is seen as the enemy.

These truly are heartbreaking situations. Mom and Dad often regard their anguished, disruptive daughter as a "bad girl"; for obvious reasons, it can be threatening to both parents to face the truth about what's making their child so unhappy. Many of these daughters become distant when they are old enough to leave home, but their problems don't go away.

It's common for these grown daughters to eventually seek the help of a therapist, because they usually have trouble forming healthy bonds with men. In therapy, these young women often become more aware of the forces that drove them away from the family. As they grow older, marry, and have children of their own, they may begin to see the dynamics between them and their parents more clearly, and to shift some of their anger away from their moms.

Mothers of these daughters often don't (or won't) recognize how badly a father's rejection can hurt. The most loving mother in the world cannot force a husband to feel affection for his daughter, which means that Mom must spend years trying single-handedly to meet both their needs—not to mention the needs of the other kids. One way to survive is to deny the problem and write the daughter off as a brat or troublemaker. Now that she is an adult, however, you'll probably have to reconsider these labels if you want to reconnect with her. The suggestions in chapter eleven, especially the forgiveness letter, can help you assure your daughter that despite any mistakes you and her father may have made in the past, you love her and want to make things better in the present.

Taking Sides in a Divorce

The fact that divorce is very common these days doesn't diminish the pain it causes children. Their world is their family, and unless the marriage has become obviously destructive or abusive, children usually don't understand why their parents are breaking up. Kids typically side with the "loser" in the divorce, that is, the one who was left. Much of the time they don't know the entire story, for example, that Mom is leaving Dad because he's fooling around. Sometimes they know the story but don't agree with the reasoning: Yes, Dad has a problem with gambling, but why doesn't Mom help him? Why does she have to walk out on him?

The bitterness caused by divorce can last for years, and it's often exacerbated by the parents' attitude toward each other after their separation. A daughter who has taken Dad's side in the divorce may develop a set of assumptions about her mother that are bolstered by her father's biases. As she grows into adulthood and is released from the constraints of the custody agreement, she may gradually slip out of her mother's life.

The mother of a daughter like this can reconnect with her, but she'll need to regain the daughter's trust. As with mothers of betrayed daughters (divorce is often seen by adult daughters as an enormous betrayal), these moms may have to concentrate on finding neutral territory where they and their daughters can get to know each other as equals. Again, the very thing that is most distressing to a mother—her daughter's distance—may be a necessary evil. Give your daughter a chance to miss you, then approach her with compassion, and the two of you can probably forge a lifelong bond.

How Could Mom Marry That Guy?

"I guess I should be thankful that she comes around at all." Janet, forty-eight, had been trying to bridge the gap between her and her daughter Martine, twenty-two. Martine had left home the day after high school graduation and saw Janet and her second husband, Mark, only on holidays.

Janet told me:

> I brought my kids up alone. Their father died when Martine was three and Josh wasn't even a year. For ten years I was maid, cook, and chauffeur, with no break and no man in my life. Then Mark and I met, and after dating a couple of years, we married. My daughter hates him, will not talk to him. I try to get them together, but she won't budge.

When a mother marries after years of celibacy and uninterrupted caretaking, her children see her in a new light. Suddenly Mom is dating, wearing makeup, getting phone calls—she's no longer the exclusive property of her children. It makes them uncomfortable to see her as a sexual being, but they can't hate her, so they hate the man who caused this change in her. In addition, because they can't bear to share her, they leave home as soon as possible.

How can a mother like Janet get her daughter back into the fold? It's not an easy trick. Martine will probably never apologize, but eventually she'll miss her family. Her mother has a tremendous advantage in that she had a very strong, loving relationship with Martine for many years. Now Janet will need to learn ways to gracefully invite Martine back home in a manner that allows her to keep face with the rest of the family. Janet needs to act as if everything is okay and all is forgiven. Her daughter may very well want to rejoin the clan but not know how to go about it without having to admit she was "wrong" about her stepfather.

As you'll see in chapter eleven, the fight over who is right or wrong keeps many mothers and daughters apart for months and sometimes years. Since there is no judge and jury who can objectively settle the issue anyway, it's up to Mom to make the first move, to forgive and forget. Neither of you has to take the blame if you can agree to disagree.

In patching things up with your distant daughter, you may have to let go of the fantasy where you, your kids, and your new husband are all one big happy family. In time they might grow fond of one another, but for now, concentrate on improving things between you and your daughter. What I advised for mothers who disapprove of their daughters' husbands is also true when your daughter disapproves of yours: She doesn't need to love him, she just needs to accept your choice. If you give her the opportunity to do this, she might eagerly take you up on it.

Mom's Money

It may sound absurd to anyone who's bitten her nails over where the next rent check is coming from, but wealthy parents and their daughters often come to much grief over the issue of money. Not that middle- and working-class daughters don't needle their parents for funds now and then, but in those cases there is a limit to how much the folks can spare, and the daughter realizes it. When the mother and father are well-to-do, the dialogue shifts to another level. The issue of "Who needs the money the most?" gets replaced by the question, "Who deserves it?" Wealthy daughters are often convinced that they have as much right to their parents' money as the parents do. They feel entitled to the good life in which they were raised.

When both parents are living, they can decide together how much money, if any, they should give their adult daughter each year. If she puts up a fuss and wants more, at least Mom and Dad can stand united against her demands. If the parents are divorced, adult daughters will often apply to each parent separately for "gifts." Where the situation gets most explosive, both in families that are very wealthy and in those that are just comfortable, is when the father dies and leaves all the money to Mom.

Sima, a woman in her late seventies, told me that her daughter began plaguing her for her inheritance within two weeks of her husband's death. "She'd call me at night, every night, and say, 'I want that money. That money's mine. Dad loved me. Dad wanted me to have it—give it to me!'" Another client, Jenny, confessed that over the past two years she had already given more than $150,000 to her daughter Alicia so she could start a business. The split between Jenny and Alicia had occurred when Jenny refused to fund her daughter's pet project, an organization for abused children:

> About six months ago, Alicia came to my home—I hadn't seen or heard from her in weeks—and sat me down. She says, "I want you to give me my inheritance now. I'm going to assign it to my foundation."
>
> "I can't do that," I said.
>
> "Why not?" she asked. "The money could be going to children who need it. You'll still have enough to live on."
>
> "You'll get my money when I'm gone," I told her.
>
> "Until then, I want to decide what to do with it myself."
>
> Well, she got very cold toward me. She really expected me to write her a check. She stood up and said, "Good-bye, Mother. When you decide to be a human being, give me a call."

Should you allow yourself to be blackmailed like this by your daughter? On paper, the answer is easy: Of course not. But in reality, many moms find the prospect of losing their daughter terrifying. *Would she really abandon me?* they wonder. *How much would it take to secure her devotion? How much do I owe her? What if I die? Will she come to my deathbed—will she be at my funeral?*

The deathbed-and-funeral scene haunts all mothers of distant daughters. It's a pity, because when they do occur, there is usually little solace in deathbed reunions. Your daughter will probably get more out of it than you will—what good does it do you to reconcile mere days before you pass away? As for your daughter being at your funeral, that too might be a comfort for her, and it might impress your friends and family, but you won't be there to appreciate the occasion.

When inheritance money comes between a mother and daughter, death is always present in the conversation. There is always the unspoken question: How much will Mom leave me, and when will I receive it? Can I get it before she dies? In order to take the guessing-game tension out of your relationship with your daughter, you might simply tell her exactly what she can expect to receive from you in the years that you are still walking this earth. (When substantial sums are involved, it's wise to arrive at the amount with the help of a financial adviser.)

If your daughter thinks your largesse isn't quite large enough and expresses her displeasure by refusing to see you, so be it. If there seems to be no way of reconnecting with her even after you've tried all the suggestions in chapter eleven, you must turn your attention to the future and release her from your thoughts for a while—possibly a long while. All mothers of distant daughters need to learn to be less vulnerable and more emotionally self-sufficient, and I've devoted chapter twelve to that topic.

She Can't Bear to See You Get Old

Women and men born between 1925 and 1940 are often called the sandwich generation, because we are poised between our children and our aging parents, sometimes caring for both. Our daughters, who watch us do all this caretaking, may be ill-prepared to assume these responsibilities when it's their turn. When a mother or father begins to show signs of frailty, some daughters don't have the fortitude to help. They may be frightened to see their parents' decline in health—it's too painful. And, of course, watching parents move into old age brings one's own mortality into sharp focus. If a daughter can't take the emotional heat, she may get out of the kitchen by refusing to deal with or visit her parents.

Victoria, seventy-seven, had always been the pillar of strength in her family and believed her example would rub off on her daughter Toni, forty-eight. But when Victoria's husband had a stroke, she found that Toni was unwilling to support or comfort her:

> We don't see each other at all now. She avoids coming to the house because she says she can't stand to see her father that way. I need her help—I'm here all alone with her disabled dad. She says I'm strong, I can survive. She doesn't realize that I've had to act strong even when I feel weak. Now I'm afraid she'll never come back, and when I die, I'll die alone.

It's very unfortunate that Toni turned out to be such a disappointment, but there are ways to encourage her to rise to the occasion. For one thing, Victoria must learn to tell Toni exactly what she needs from her, and to admit out loud that she can't handle this crisis alone. Strong moms such as Victoria sometimes find it very difficult to make this admission, but only by confessing your limitations will you be able to convince others that you really do need their help.

By the same token, Victoria must accept Toni's limitations. Her daughter may not be able to provide her with the kind of unwavering attention Victoria feels she deserves. Victoria—and all older moms—need to chart out a future for themselves while they still have the energy and capabilities to do so. In chapter twelve I'll tell you the kinds of prep work you can do now to plan for the various turns your life may take in your later years. When you feel that you are in control of your life and have prepared for your future, you can approach your daughter with more confidence. You can ask her for help in specific areas—for instance, researching senior centers or medical plans—rather than coming across to her as a mass of undefined needs.

It may not seem fair that your daughter lacks your sense of duty or emotional strength. But we must recognize, too, that our daughters have family and work obligations that can't be forsaken the moment we need them at our side. Adjust your expectations to fit reality, and your reluctant daughter may summon the courage to be there for you when it counts. But remember, nowhere is it written that your children are obligated to help you—it is a choice they make of their own free will.

When Your Daughter Is Ashamed of You

America is a nation of immigrants, and wherever there is an immigrant mom with an accent, unusual clothes, and ethnic food, you can bet there's a daughter who's ashamed of her. Other daughters are ashamed of their parents' values, social status, or lack of education. Many deal with their embarrassment by distancing themselves from Mom and Dad and the old neighborhood. They breeze in on Christmas, Passover, or Thanksgiving, bearing expensive gifts and tales from the big city. Then they are gone again, as inaccessible as a career girl on a TV sitcom.

Lydia, fifty-six, told me that her daughter had sailed through college on a wave of scholarships and awards but didn't encourage her parents to celebrate her achievements with her:

> She's a graduate of Radcliffe, and her dad and I barely completed high school. She lived in a sorority and earned every scholarship available at the time. A National Merit Scholar is pretty special, and here we are living in a bad neighborhood in Boston, her dad driving a cab. I've invited

her over for dinner many times, but she always has some lame excuse. I've never met any of her college friends; in fact, we didn't even attend her graduation for fear we would embarrass her. What will happen when she marries? Will I meet her fiancé? Will we even be invited to the wedding?

Lydia, like most of these moms, seemed to accept her daughter's embarrassment as the price she had to pay for having a successful, upwardly mobile daughter. In many immigrant cultures, too, a well-assimilated child is the ultimate status symbol; Mom may feel she has no right to complain when her daughter has triumphed so gloriously in the new country. But for her daughter's sake as much as her own, a mother must overcome her sense of inadequacy and reach out to her estranged child. She deserves a place in her daughter's life, and her daughter needs a mother, whether or not she admits it to herself right now.

The distant daughter who is ashamed of her parents will come to regret it if she doesn't eventually reconnect with them. In the worst-case scenario, the mother or father dies before the daughter has reestablished ties with them. The daughter's grief is deep and inconsolable, and her guilt may last the rest of her life. Many distant daughters wrestle daily with guilt about hiding their parents and background from their contemporaries. But they've gotten used to the deceit, so until a crisis occurs they continue the truncated, holidays-only relationship—unless Mom insists on something better.

Mothers who feel unworthy of their daughters' time and attention will benefit greatly from the advice I give in chapter twelve about joining support groups and expanding your activities within your community. By widening your horizons this way, you'll build up enough self-confidence to approach your daughter as an equal, not a supplicant. Then you can use some of the techniques from chapter nine to establish safe, neutral territory for you and her to relax in.

With a distant daughter, finding neutral territory might mean meeting her halfway—literally. If she's unwilling to invite you to her house or to come "all the way out there" to visit you, meet halfway. If she's embarrassed about the way you dress, suggest that she go shopping with you and together you can buy "daughter clothes," an outfit you'll wear when you're in her company. In theory your daughter should love you just the way you are, but in reality you'll have to make some compromises in order to spend more time with her. Meanwhile, you can take comfort in the likelihood that as she matures, your daughter may learn to move more gracefully between her two worlds: the one that nourished her, and the one in which she now thrives.

What Your Daughter Leaves Behind

When a daughter breaks off from her family, the damage she does is profound. In many ways, it's like a death. Sometimes the break is abrupt and obvious, as when a daughter moves and leaves her parents no forwarding address or phone number. In other instances her withdrawal is gradual, which is why it takes some mothers as long as six or seven years to realize what has happened. When they finally understand, they often enter into a state of perpetual grief.

Some of the mothers I counsel don't know if their daughter is dead or alive; whether she's married or has children; if she's safe, or suffering, or homeless. Every day they ask themselves, *I wonder where she is?* Or *Damn her! How could she do this to us?* There is no relief from the pain, and it ripples out to affect every area of a mother's life, beginning with her marriage.

Grief doesn't necessarily bind a man and woman together. Instead, it often happens that both partners are so bereaved they have nothing left to offer each other. And because the daughter chose to leave, there's always the question of who's to blame for her disappearance. Who displeased her so much that she'd cut off the entire family? The other siblings, if there are any, are hurt and angry because she's left them, too. In essence she's said, "I don't approve of any of you. I don't need or want you, so I'm leaving." That's a terrible insult.

If the parents manage to hold their marriage together in the wake of this awful crisis, they still must contend with their friends and relatives, all of whom ask about the missing daughter. Mom and Dad at some point make a decision either to downplay the situation or, in some cases, to lie about it. Either choice is emotionally wracking.

One client of mine, Olivia, had a daughter who moved out of her college town and left no clue as to her destination. Olivia, fifty-eight, was brokenhearted, but she still holds fast to the belief that in time her daughter Cindy will contact her. Until then, Olivia and her husband have invented a whole life for Cindy for public consumption.

> I tell people that Cindy works in Ankara, Turkey, at an archeological institute. Why Ankara? Because nobody I know visits there, so there's no chance our friends will want to get in touch with her while they're on vacation. Last summer my husband and I went to Europe, and when we came back we told everyone we'd had a wonderful holiday with Cindy. No one knows the truth. It's horrible, but what am I going to say—that I don't know where my daughter is?

For mothers who choose to downplay their daughters' absence rather than fib about it, conversations with friends can become stilted and painful. When asked about her daughter, a mom will offer brief, noncommittal answers and then quickly change the subject. The conversations are awkward for her friends as well. They don't want to cause her pain, so they try not to discuss their own children. Here too there is a similarity to the way people deal with death: the strongest friends step up and support you, while those with less emotional fortitude withdraw.

Many moms find conversing with their friends so stressful that they begin to gravitate toward people who are childless and won't be as likely to question them about their daughter. The company of these people provides a respite, and there is nothing at all wrong with that. I mention it only to point out the extent to which a daughter's absence can affect her mother's daily life.

And then there are the mothers who disappear when their child disappears. They stop socializing altogether and their world dwindles to a sad and isolated routine. They obsess on what they have lost: not only their daughter but their grandchildren. The guilt and loneliness are tremendous. These are the women who tell me, "I regret being a parent" or "I've stopped caring; a part of me has died."

But even though you have lost your child, you have not lost you. You must hold on to your own sense of identity and purpose. You can't let yourself become a casualty of your daughter's disappearance. Always remember that you are not just a mother, you are a person. You can make a life for yourself that has pleasure in it, even as you bear this grievous loss.

Every mother can benefit from adjusting her outlook so that her children are a joyous part of her life but not the maypole around which everything revolves. In chapter twelve I'll share with you the insights of clients who have moved from mourning a missing daughter to enjoying an active and satisfying life. Before I do, however, I want to give you every tool I know of to get your daughter back. "Never give up hope," I tell mothers of distant daughters. "Where there is love, there is hope."

CHAPTER ELEVEN

Raising the White Flag

I haven't seen my daughter face-to-face for six years. I passed by
her at a wedding a month ago, and she nodded. I want to know
what I did wrong. How can I correct our problem? After all this
time, will she ever want to talk to me again?

— *A d e l e ,   a g e   s i x t y - f o u r*

In 1994, Los Angeles suffered a massive earthquake.
Walls fell off the sides of buildings, chimneys crumbled, and
whole structures collapsed to the foundation. After the first days
of panic subsided, I got the urge to drive past some of the ruined
buildings. As I looked at all those fallen structures, I noticed how,
even if a building lay exposed and broken, the foundation beneath
it always seemed to survive intact.

The love between a mother and daughter is like the foundation
of those buildings. Submerged, neglected for years, it's still there
even if the relationship appears to have crumbled. Mothers will
often say to me, "I still love her. I don't like her, I hate what she's
doing, but underneath it all I'm still her mother." That's the spirit
that can salvage your broken relationship with your daughter.

I won't pretend it's easy. Of all the moms I counsel, those with
distant daughters suffer the most and must overcome the steepest

obstacles. The methods I describe in this book are not an immediate fix, but if you're tenacious enough, they offer you a good
chance of getting your distant daughter back.

To make the best of the advice in these pages, pay attention to
the way you're feeling each step of the way. It's entirely appropriate to be sad or depressed at times during this program, but don't
keep your sadness to yourself; talk to a friend or read a chapter
together with a loved one. We are all vulnerable, and we all need
to be shored up when we're making a major change like this.
Doing it alone only makes the process more difficult than it has
to be.

While it may not always be a pleasure to follow the steps I've
laid out, they are all aimed toward positive goals: to reunite with
your daughter and to gain some peace and serenity in your life
whether or not your attempts to reconcile succeed. You must look inward
to gain that peace, and you must be honest with yourself.

Reconciling with your daughter may be a slow, arduous
process, but by the same token it might go more quickly than you
dreamed possible, especially if she is longing to reconnect but
doesn't have the courage to make the first move. In this chapter
I'm going to show you how to approach her, how to find a therapist or mediator to ensure that your meetings with her don't go
up in flames, and how to maintain your new relationship.

Reviewing Your Past

Part I of this book is essential reading for any mother, but it's particularly helpful for mothers of distant daughters. Since your
daughter is not around to talk things over with, you must look
inward for clues as to how your relationship faltered. When you
do connect with her and start working through your problems,
you'll need to be able to speak honestly about your perception of
the past and your old expectations of her.

If you read Part I but didn't take the time to do the exercises in chapter three, I strongly urge you to do them now. You don't have to schedule a marathon exercise-taking session; on the contrary, don't rush it. Pick one exercise, settle down with a cup of tea, and allow yourself enough time to thoughtfully answer the questions. It may take you a few hours to complete each exercise, so don't plan on doing more than one a day. As you answer the questions, reflect on how your behavior, expectations, or the events in your shared past could have contributed to your daughter's bad feelings about you and the family.

You'll learn a lot about yourself if you answer the questions truthfully, and it can take some time for you to absorb those insights. In psychological terms this process is called *integrating*—becoming comfortable with a new set of ideas. If you try to integrate too much at once, you'll overtax yourself and the work won't be as effective as it will if you let the ideas sink in slowly. So take it one exercise at a time, and if you need two weeks to complete them all, that's fine. At the end of that time, you will have gained some perspective on your troubles with your daughter.

During these few weeks of intense introspection, treat yourself kindly. No matter what mistakes you made, if you loved your daughter and tried to do right by her, you still qualify as a good person and a good mom. The point of all this reflection is not to heap more blame upon yourself, but to look at your relationship objectively. If you start to feel blue or guilty or hopeless, shut the book and go do something diverting—see a movie, have lunch with a friend, get a massage. In a day or two, when you're feeling up to it, go back to the exercise.

The wish list you write at the end of chapter three spells out your hopes for your new relationship with your daughter. It is based on your revised expectations and is possibly the most worthwhile exercise this book will demand of you. Any success you hope to have with your daughter depends on your being able to accept her for who she is, and that means revising your expectations to fit reality.

Your Daughter's State of Mind

A mother who hasn't been in close contact with her daughter will sometimes balk at the idea of simply accepting her. For one thing, Mom's not exactly sure who her daughter is anymore. Is she the sloppy rebel who hid drugs in her desk drawer and sneaked out her window at night? The sullen bookworm who wouldn't shave her legs or date boys? The resentful good girl who developed anorexia rather than stand up to her mother?

Your adult daughter is none of these. Although you may remember her high school years with particular intensity, your daughter has grown and changed since she left home. Her lifestyle may be dramatically different from yours, but that doesn't mean it is wrong. If you're going to patch things up with her, you must try to view her objectively and not as an extension or reflection of you.

When she sought my advice, Beth, fifty-three, hadn't seen her daughter Andi, twenty-seven, in ten years. Beth had cast Andi out of her home on the night of her senior prom, when the girl dropped a bombshell on her family:

> Andi and I had shopped for a prom dress together but in the end she said she'd buy her own outfit. She kept her date a secret, too. It was all very mysterious, but nothing could have prepared me for what happened.
>
> About seven o'clock the doorbell rings and Andi rushes through the living room to answer it. We barely had time to register that she wasn't wearing a gown, but a tuxedo. A few minutes go by; we hear whispering. My husband and I still had no idea what was up.
>
> Suddenly she walks into the room arm in arm with her best friend, Jeanne. "Mom and Dad, this is my date," she says. "We're in love."

Within seconds all four of us were screaming at each other—the room just exploded. Finally I told her, "Get out of this house. We'll discuss this tomorrow." I was so astonished and hurt—it seemed as if she had planned it this way just to outrage us. To this day, I still believe the whole prom mess was intended to shock us.

We never got to talk the next day because she was already gone. She had figured out that we'd be furious and had planned her escape up to San Francisco. When she called six months later, I hung up on her.

A large part of Beth's lingering anger at her daughter had to do with her suspicion that Andi's prom-night revelation was an intentional attack on her mother and father. In the years that followed, Andi tried to contact her mother a few times, but every conversation sank under Beth's accusations: "Why did you humiliate me? Everyone in town knows what you did." Beth didn't consider other possible reasons for Andi's behavior, which came to light when she and Andi finally met in my office. As it turned out, Andi had been tormented by her fear of telling her parents she was gay, and her girlfriend, Jeanne, had pressured her to make prom night a grand gesture of their passion. Since Andi had no better idea how to break the news, she agreed to the "prom-night massacre," as she called it.

In the ten years following Andi's flight, Beth had grown to miss her daughter terribly. Although she still disapproved of her gay lifestyle, Beth was aching to get back in touch with Andi. At the time she first came to see me, she and Andi had begun to speak more often, but the conversations were awkward and heavy with unspoken feelings.

In order to set the stage for rapprochement, I suggested that Beth try to put aside her judgments about Andi's sexuality for a few moments and gauge her daughter's personality objectively, as a therapist would. Beth had great difficulty seeing Andi's choices as anything other than a reaction against the family. Getting an objective view of her daughter's life was essential to Beth's being able to accept Andi as an adult, not a rebellious teenager.

I gave Beth the following list of questions, which you, too, should ask yourself about your daughter. If you haven't seen her in a while, you can think back to the way she behaved when you were in closer touch with her. You can also ask family members who are in contact with her now to tell you a little about how your daughter is functioning.

Your Daughter: A Mental Status Review

- Does your daughter have a job, a car, a decent domicile?
- Does your daughter have a spouse or significant other?
- Does your daughter have friendships that she sustains?
- Does your daughter have the ability to feel pleasure and pain?
- Does your daughter have interests or hobbies?
- Does your daughter appear to miss you and her family?
- Is your daughter free of addictions?
- Is your daughter a mother, and if so, is she raising healthy, happy children?

Now, this is not exactly a clinical evaluation. It's more a device to get you to step back and see your daughter the way a disinterested third party would. If you answered yes to all or most of these questions, your daughter is probably a healthy, functioning adult. She may be eccentric, she may not hold a job you respect, she may be with a man or woman of whom you disapprove, but objectively speaking she is mentally stable. Given that fact, she ought to be able to sit down and have a reasonable meeting with you. But you must realize that when and if she does agree to meet, you will not be in a position to criticize her about her life choices. She's a functioning adult, and so are you—two grown individuals getting to know each other again.

Control Your Desire to Control Your Daughter

Liberal acceptance is at the heart of everything I have to teach mothers about their daughters. When you open up and accept your daughter for who she is, you'll also be open to creating a new kind of relationship with her. Just as there are different types of daughters, there are different types of relationships, and no type is better than another. Mothers who think there is an ideal, one-size-fits-all relationship are bound to be disappointed. As they try to force their daughter to conform to that impossible ideal, she will recoil. Conversely, if a mother can accept her daughter as is and let go of her desire to shape and control the relationship, the odds of improving it become much better.

If you are a controlling mom, your first task is to admit it to yourself. As I mentioned in the last chapter, it often takes moms six months or so to face up to this aspect of themselves; prior to that, they'll concede to being opinionated, strong-willed, forceful, a take-charge personality . . . anything but overbearing or controlling. Once you do acknowledge this unappealing attribute, you can tackle the ultimate challenge: controlling yourself.

Every time you feel the need to be in control of other people, immediately ask yourself why. *Why do I need to choose the restaurant, select the table, tell everyone where to sit, and suggest what they all order? Why must I be in charge?* Most overbearing people need to control others because they feel chaotic inside. Unless they command all aspects of their environment, they become anxious. Moms such as this are accustomed to steamrollering their families; after twenty or thirty years, the other members usually respond with a weary, "Whatever you say, Ma." Everyone, that is, except the distant daughter, who chooses to flee rather than be flattened.

In order to start anew with your daughter, you will have to curb your controlling behavior. You can practice on other people, so that when you meet with her you'll be good at holding your tongue. In addition, memorize the five most irritating things mothers do, which I discussed in chapter eight. Controlling mothers are often guilty of all five of them, so:

1. Stop interrogating her.
2. Stop invading her privacy.
3. Stop judging her by the way you live.
4. Stop criticizing her for being innately different from you.
5. Stop giving her unsolicited advice.

Making the Most Out of Distance

Although the aim of this book is to bring you closer to your daughter, there may be a silver lining to the distance between you right now. For one thing, either you or your daughter must have felt the break was necessary for emotional survival. If your daughter was causing you such worry and pain that you asked her not to call for a while, that was probably a healthy move. Similarly, if she left because she couldn't stand the stress of the relationship, perhaps it was a wise choice for her. Another benefit to distance is that it gives you and your daughter a chance to miss each other. If you don't miss each other, you won't have the incentive to see the rapprochement through.

Sometimes it only takes a few months for the rancor to dissolve and the missing stage to set in. Cecilia, seventy-seven, had angrily decreed that her two daughters were not to call or visit her anymore after they both refused to take time off from work to escort her cross-country to visit her ill sister (Cecilia's brother eventually came to her rescue). But several months later she relented; it was the Fourth of July, and they had always celebrated with a big family cookout. Cecilia longed to see her daughters but was worried that they'd want to punish her for casting them out. On the contrary, they were both delighted to hear from their mother when she called. No one mentioned the argument, and they didn't need to. They all missed one another and wanted to get back together.

If yours is a more serious rift, you can make use of the time away from your daughter to review your past, revise your expectations, and begin making changes in your behavior. The more insight you gain during the period of estrangement, the more likely it is that your new relationship will work. And let's face it, something wasn't working before or your daughter wouldn't be gone. If it's not all her fault—and it rarely is—you are part of the problem, and you're going to need to change in order to get her back.

Before You Reach Out to Your Daughter

In addition to revising your expectations and learning to change some of your behavior, there are three promises you must make to yourself as you prepare to reconnect with your daughter.

Forget about who is right and who is wrong. "It's not fair! It's unjust, what she did to me." The issue of right and wrong seems to stick in the side of mothers like a thorn, poisoning their efforts to make peace with their daughters. Unless you are willing to let go of those old grudges and injustices, you can forget about a successful reconciliation. You believe you are right, and your daughter believes she is. The most you can do is agree to disagree and move on from there.

Instead of nursing your old grievances against your daughter, imagine that you are placing them all in a metal lock box like the ones they keep in the bank vault. Then imagine that you are taking the box, boarding a row boat, and rowing to the middle of the nearest lake. Dump the box in the lake, and visualize it sinking to the bottom. Watch as the silt and sand drift over it, and feel the water cool the anger of all those grudges. Then turn the boat around and row back to shore.

When you meet with your daughter you'll probably discuss the past; there's no way around it. The conversation will be a lot more productive if your anger over her injustices has cooled. Always bear in mind that the point of your meeting is to create a new relationship, not wrest an apology from her, and that your grudges are at the bottom of a lake.

Forgive your daughter and ask her to forgive you. In the next section of this chapter I describe the forgiveness letter, in which a mother writes and asks her daughter to forgive her for any pain, intentional or not, that the mother may have caused. Whether you write a forgiveness letter or express the sentiments in person, it is crucial that you ask your daughter's forgiveness. By doing so you accept your culpability in the rift and acknowledge that without your daughter's good will, no meaningful reunion can take place. At the same time, you must be prepared to forgive her for any pain she caused you and the family, whether intentional or not.

Listen with an open mind and heart to what your daughter tells you. If you are able to put aside your old grievances and ask for your daughter's forgiveness, you'll probably be in a receptive enough state of mind to hear what she has to say to you when you meet—but brace yourself, for you will be criticized. Most of us become defensive when that happens; it's a natural reaction. In order to work through your problems, you'll have to keep your defensiveness in check so you can learn what your daughter is so angry about.

The White Flag and the Forgiveness Letter

Once you've integrated the new ideas in this book, you'll be ready to approach your distant daughter. Most parents know where their daughter lives, but there are those who have lost contact with her altogether. If that's the case with you, there are several ways you can learn her whereabouts. The most obvious is to check with your relatives until you find one who's privy to the information. Sometimes your other children know; sometimes it's a cousin or aunt. If your daughter has instructed the family member not to divulge her address, you can have them mail a letter for you.

Only rarely does a child cut off contact with the entire extended family, but if your daughter has done so, you can always hire a detective to locate her. If you have a date of birth, social security number, and driver's license number, there is a decent chance the detective will be successful, but they make no promises. The more pieces of paper the detective has to work with, the better. Beware, however, of detectives who claim they can find anyone in seventy-two hours—they're usually charlatans.

When you have your daughter's address (and, ideally, a phone number) in hand, you can make your move. If the conflict between a mother and daughter is painful but not terribly traumatic, I often suggest that Mom send her daughter a white flag, the international symbol of surrender. The flag means, "I don't want to fight anymore, so let's put away the weapons and sit down at the treaty table." The flag can be a handkerchief or a square of white cloth. With it you can send a very brief note: "Truce? Let's talk. Love, Mom."

The white flag can be a terrific icebreaker—it's funny and it relays your willingness to admit you were at least partly in the wrong. In some cases, however, the white flag is inappropriate. Some rifts are too serious to be trivialized by this gesture, no matter how well-intentioned it is. In those situations I recommend sending your daughter a forgiveness letter. It should read something like this:

Dear _____,

> I want so badly to reconcile with you. I miss you so much, and I love you.
>
> If at any time I have inadvertently hurt your feelings, I ask your forgiveness.
>
> If at any time I have harmed you by the things I've done or failed to do, I ask your forgiveness.
>
> If I have ever neglected or abused you, I ask your forgiveness.
>
> If I have been a disappointment to you, I ask your forgiveness.
>
> I want to have a loving relationship with you, and to attain that I will do whatever is necessary. Please help me.
>
> I need your forgiveness.
>
> Your loving mom

This is a powerful letter to write and an extraordinary one to receive. In your lifetime you may never compose a more intensely meaningful letter than this, and I realize that it's very difficult to do. If you need a little extra strength to pen these words, consider turning to the Bible, particularly Luke. In Luke 6:37, Jesus says, "Judge not, and ye shall not be judged: condemn not, and ye shall not be condemned: forgive, and ye shall be forgiven." Luke 7:39–50 is also food for thought. There, Jesus explains to Simon the connection between love and forgiveness:

> **"There was a certain creditor which had two debtors: One owed five hundred pence, and the other fifty. And when**

they had nothing to pay, he frankly forgave them both. Tell me therefore, which of them will love him the most?" Simon answered and said that *he,* to whom he forgave the most. And he said unto him, "Thou hast rightly judged."

Contact!

About a week after you send the white flag or forgiveness letter, follow it up with a phone call (if you have your daughter's number). When you talk to her you can suggest getting together along with a mediator, as I describe later in this chapter. If you don't have her number and she doesn't write or call, or if she hangs up on you, don't get discouraged. It often takes several tries before a daughter will let down her defenses. Keep writing to her intermittently, but don't deluge her with mail. Send her cards on holidays and her birthday, with brief messages such as "I love you and miss you. Please write or call, anytime." A card on Mother's Day can be especially effective if you include a note that is loving but not guilt-inducing, such as "The happiest day of my life was when you were born. You taught me how to be a mother—thank you."

If your daughter is not receptive to your first attempts, use the intervening time to learn about yourself and improve your outlook. One of the best ways to do this is to join a mother's group (more about those in chapter twelve) and listen to the experiences of other moms.

These groups can work miracles. Time and again mothers have come into my mothers' groups looking like the walking wounded, their heads down, their expressions flat and hopeless. When I ask them to talk about their distant daughter, they say, "I've never told anybody about it because I'm so ashamed."

"Ashamed of what?" I ask.

"Ashamed that my daughter and I don't talk to each other. Ashamed of my part in it."

In a mothers' group you can finally break your silence and end that awful isolation. And, while no group can erase your past mistakes, it can allow you to see how human those mistakes were. After hearing the stories of other moms, you might view your own errors less harshly. You'll learn from their experiences and be able to apply their insights to your situation. Best of all, you'll have continual emotional support from people who understand what you're going through.

Sooner or later, in the majority of cases, the distant daughter does respond to her mother's letters. By the time that happens, you should be ready to suggest a plan for rapprochement. You could meet together, just the two of you, but I strongly advise against that. With distant daughters it is much safer and smarter to meet with a third person, a mediator who can help diffuse the anger and keep the discussion on track.

When the phone call you've been waiting for finally arrives, try to stay calm. Naturally you'll be delighted to hear from your daughter, but don't scare her away with demands or questions. Keep the conversation warm but, for lack of a better word, businesslike. After the initial greetings, which will probably be a little awkward, you might say:

> **I'm so pleased to hear from you. I've been thinking about the mistakes I've made in the past, and I think it would be wonderful if you and I could get together and talk, along with a mediator. I don't want to get off on the wrong foot with you, and I really feel that we need someone objective to help us bridge the gap between us. Would you be interested in doing this?**

If your daughter has worked up the courage to contact you, she'll probably be open to the idea of a meeting. Involving a mediator takes away some of the danger; it won't be just the two of you facing off. If she seems willing to listen to your plan, you can segue right into the next topic: choosing a mediator and setting a date.

Why Use a Mediator?

People who have never been to a professional counselor are sometimes leery about involving an outsider in their personal problems. They're afraid they'll be embarrassed, humiliated, and worst of all, judged: "You lied to your daughter? Oh, you're a bad person" or "You neglected your mother? Shame on you!"

This is not how it works. Your mediator—usually a member of the clergy or a therapist—is not out to judge or condemn you but to make it easier for you and your daughter to talk to each other. No ethical mediator is going to pass judgment on what you are feeling or thinking. In fact, one of the oft-repeated tenets of psychology is that feelings aren't right or wrong, they just *are.* If you feel furious about something that your daughter is sad about, that's because you and she have different perceptions of the same problem. And when you reveal these feelings to the counselor, she'll probably say, "You're both right—neither one of you is wrong. Now, let's see how we can resolve this."

Gloria, sixty-two, and her daughter Amy, thirty, provide a good example of the mediation process at work. Gloria complained that Amy was selfish and short-tempered, while Amy complained that her mother was too controlling. To illustrate her point, Amy recounted what happened when they tried to attend an art fair together:

> Before she'd agree to go, Mom had to know exactly when we were leaving, when we were coming back, where we were going to park, how many people would be there, was it indoors or out. Finally I couldn't take it anymore and told her to forget it. I don't have the time to root out all that information for her. Why can't she just go along with the program?

During the course of our session, I asked Gloria why the logistics were so important to her. She finally admitted that the crowds made her very nervous because she was overweight and had a hard time moving quickly. "I get scared that something will happen—like a fire—and I won't be able to get out." Like most daughters, Amy was accustomed to viewing her mother as a parent, not a person; she only saw her mother's behavior in terms of how it affected her, Amy. *She wants all that information so she can control the outing and me.* In reality, Gloria's nervousness had nothing to do with controlling Amy.

This sort of insight happens frequently in a therapeutic setting. It's not that Gloria and Amy are too ignorant to figure things out for themselves but that they are too enmeshed in the dynamic to see their problems clearly. Therapists are schooled to pick up on their clients' underlying motives; equally important, we stand outside the relationship so we can see it objectively.

It's nearly impossible for two estranged people to achieve this objectivity by themselves. They're too angry to scrutinize their own behavior, and too hurt and impatient to hear the other person out. They lack the mutual trust it takes to do any intense soul-searching together. To make matters worse, they can't articulate their feelings in a productive way. Instead, conversations tend to blow up as both mother and daughter fall back into their old patterns of communication. A mediator guides you through the rough patches, metabolizes the bad feelings, and can lead you to revelations you'd never have on your own. For distant daughters and their mothers, using a mediator offers the best odds for rapprochement.

Finding a Good Therapist

One of my daughters lives near Gridley, California, a tiny hamlet with a population of about twelve hundred. The downtown is all of four square blocks, but as I walked the streets there one day, I saw that, sure enough, they had a counseling center.

Consider yourself lucky that today it's easy to find help no matter where you live or how much money you have. Communities have become very enlightened in this area, and many of them offer counseling services at no charge or for a nominal fee. You can get excellent help from these centers, which are usually staffed by a combination of interns, professionals doing pro bono work, and experienced paraprofessional therapists.

To locate a therapist in your town, simply phone the United Way and ask for its Info Line. The Info Line operator will provide you with a list of options ranging from low- or no-fee counselors, to higher priced therapists, to support groups. The support groups are great for moms by themselves, but for the meetings with your daughter I recommend private sessions with a counselor.

If you've been in therapy before, you can always seek that therapist's help again. She already knows your history, which makes the process go more quickly. But don't do this without consulting your daughter; she may prefer that you use her therapist or one who doesn't know either of you yet. (By the way, you and your daughter should split the therapist's fee in order to maintain a balance of power.)

If you don't like the first therapist you meet with, by all means try a different one! You must both be comfortable with this person for the process to work. Sometimes a therapist will just rub you the wrong way, in which case you should not continue with her. Don't worry about insulting her; it's an occupational hazard to which we therapists are accustomed.

It's also possible that the therapist will remind you of someone you don't like. That happened to me—I reminded my client of her mother-in-law. "You talk just like her, you have the same coloring, and she's from New Jersey, too," she told me. We finally agreed that it wasn't going to work; she loathed her mother-in-law and as a result had a lot of trouble opening up to me.

It shouldn't take you and your daughter more than two or three therapists to find one you can both work with. (If you can't seem to agree on anyone, ask yourselves how serious you are about the process.) Most people can get a feel for a therapist over the phone; interview several of them, have your daughter do the same, and then decide on a date and time for your first meeting.

Just the Three of Us: Your First Meeting with Your Daughter and the Therapist

You, your daughter, and the therapist will spend most of your first session getting to know one another. The therapist will do some basic information gathering, perhaps asking where you and your daughter reside, where you were raised, whether or not you're married, if you have other children, where you work, and so forth. There is another, more subtle exchange going on in this first meeting: the therapist is trying to establish a rapport with you, trying to let you know that she cares about you and your problems. This caring is a fundamental part of therapy, because the success of the program depends on trust. You and your daughter must feel as if the therapist understands you and can identify with your issues.

Having worked with mothers and daughters for many years, I've developed some basic guidelines that help keep the reconciliation process on track. I'll share these guidelines with you now, but they're not carved in stone. All therapists have their own style of working. Ultimately you must select one based on a combination of hunch and intellect: Do you like the person, and do his or her methods seem reasonable to you? If so, take the plunge.

Provided we all get along in the first meeting, I generally ask my clients to commit to a six-session contract. The sessions can take place once a week, every other week, once a month—whatever is feasible for both mother and daughter. I've found that it takes at least six sessions to get beyond "She made me wear orthopedic shoes" and "She never lifted a hand to help me." Beneath these superficial complaints are the real culprits: issues of control, expectations, betrayal, mistrust. If mother and daughter need a breather after the first six sessions, I suggest that we take a hiatus and reconvene in a month or two. If not much has been accomplished after session six, I advise my clients to commit to another six sessions.

I don't believe that therapy should go on forever. Many of my mothers and daughters stay with me for a year, then take some time off to integrate their new insights and practice what they've learned. In another six months or a year, if they're so inclined, they return to learn more. In a sense, therapy is like school: it teaches you how to live your life better, and you can take that as far as you like.

There are four basic rules I ask mothers and daughters to follow while they're in a session with me.

1. *Define your goals.* Mothers who've read this book have already fine-tuned their goals back in chapter three, when they wrote their wish list. Your goals in therapy should be specific, such as "I want to be able to visit with my daughter and not have my stomach knot up in fear."

When asked what their goals are, I've had many clients reply, "I want to be happy." *I want to be happy* is not a goal; it's an existential dilemma. Philosophers can ponder the big questions about human happiness; therapists need something more concrete to work with.

2. *No interrupting (also known as the gag rule).* When the other person is talking, do not under any circumstances interrupt her. If your daughter makes a comment you'd like to respond to, take notes. When it's your turn to speak, she will listen quietly to your response.

3. *Agree to disagree.* Therapy will not give you "closure" on the events that drove you apart, nor will your therapist decree whose version of the past is correct. You're in therapy to learn how to deal with your perceptions and feelings, not to proclaim a winner. You will not be in agreement about your shared history;

the most you can do is agree to disagree and try to move on to a better relationship.

4. *Understand that change comes slowly.* A rift that's lasted for years won't be healed in a session or two of counseling, although you might be amazed at what you can accomplish once you start being truthful about your feelings. Still, it takes time to trust each other enough to let down your defenses, time to integrate new ideas, and time to accept each other as adults and individuals. So don't be impatient—stay committed to the process.

What If Your Daughter Lives out of Town?

It's common for distant daughters to move far away from their hometown for the sole purpose of avoiding their family. Even so, you can use the methods in this book to bridge the gap between you and your daughter. The process may take longer to reach fruition, but you'll still be making progress.

Follow all the steps described in this chapter, including sending a white flag or forgiveness letter and following up with cards or notes. As soon as your daughter responds, you can move on to the next level: planning a visit to her.

This visit will be different from any you've previously taken, in that you will plan it all out without involving your daughter. Make tentative arrangements for your flight, transportation, and lodging before telling her you're coming. Since you want this trip to be as stress-free as possible, *do not stay with your daughter.* Spend the night at another relative's house or book a room in a nearby hotel or bed-and-breakfast. Saving money is not the point of this visit, so don't let any penny-pinching tendencies get the better of you. Even if your daughter assumes you'll be sleeping in her spare room, gently decline her offer unless you're truly too strapped to afford a hotel.

Why is it so important to find separate accommodations? First, it relieves your daughter of the pressure of having to get the house ready for you (read: clean it to your standards). Second, sleeping under the same roof may be too much, too soon—it could set off a chain reaction of old bad habits that might sabotage the visit. Third, staying on your own allows you to act independently from your daughter so that the two of you can maintain a balance of power. Finally, if you're not staying in her house, there is nothing she can do to prevent you from coming.

Don't ask your daughter if you can visit; she'll probably say, "It's not a good time." Instead make it clear that you *will* be coming— "I miss you terribly and I've made up my mind to come see you"—and suggest several possible dates. Assure your daughter that you'll handle the details of the trip yourself, including renting a car at the airport or taking a cab to the hotel. You must be as self-sufficient as you possibly can on this first visit, and probably on many visits thereafter.

If your daughter seems guardedly optimistic about the trip, ask her permission to set up a meeting between you, her, and a counselor. Since it's her city, she may know of a good therapist; otherwise, you can do the footwork over the telephone just as you would in your own town. If she rejects the notion of seeing a counselor, no harm done: you've planted the seed in her mind. You'll just have to take what you've learned from this book and apply it as best you can on your own. The next time you visit, you can again suggest a counseling session. Eventually she may agree to it.

"Why do I have to do all the planning?" mothers will protest when I lay out this strategy. It's simple: If you don't do it, your daughter probably won't either. White flags, cards, and forgiveness letters can get you only so far—sooner or later you must see your daughter face-to-face in order to rebuild the bond. You are the mother, the older one, the wiser one. Show her how much she means to you by making the effort to see her; let her learn by your example. If you wait for your daughter to do "her share," you may be waiting forever.

Take this book with you on your trip for comfort and inspiration. If you do nothing else, memorize the five most irritating things mothers do and swear to yourself that you will not do them! In the hotel at night, read chapters one through three again to remind yourself of why you became a mom and what you can reasonably expect from your daughter.

Once you've arrived in town, start out with a brief visit that lasts perhaps an hour or two. It's ideal if you can see your daughter alone, but if she wants the emotional support of her mate and children, graciously consent. You don't have to get your way about everything; instead, go along with her, be flexible. If your first meeting goes smoothly, plan another for the next day, but be careful not to overdo it. You are both on slippery footing, and the time you spend together may be emotionally exhausting. That's another good reason for staying in a hotel—you can recuperate in private and gear yourself up for the next interaction. While you're at it, avail yourself of the hotel's Jacuzzi and ask the concierge what the city has to offer. You've come all this way, so why not have a little fun?

Don't expect this first visit to undo all the strangeness and anger of the past years. This is a beginning, the first step in a process that will go on for the rest of your life. When you go back home, continue to send your daughter cards, a letter now and then, maybe a bouquet of flowers on a special occasion. And when the time is right, plan your second visit. Every step you take will bring you closer to your daughter; every time you reach out to her, you'll know you're doing all you can to make up for the past.

Care and Maintenance of Your New Relationship

I often say that the bond between mother and daughter is unbreakable, and I believe that it is. But when the bond has been torn, as it has with distant daughters, it will always require special care. Scar tissue will replace the tear, but scar tissue is fragile—the wound can open again. So take nothing for granted with your daughter, and never assume that your work with her is done. There are always holidays, crises, family events that will test your new relationship, and you have to be prepared for them.

There are really only two ground rules to remember as you embark on this lifelong rebonding: Respect each other and stay committed to the process. Even if it gets uncomfortable—and it will—see it through. Even when you learn things you never wanted to know about yourself, your family, and your daughter, somehow find the will to persevere.

Because I know that mothers and their distant daughters inevitably hit rough spots, I generally have them schedule a checkup session with me even when they're finished with therapy. I'll ask them to set a date perhaps four months into the future, just so we can all sit down together and untangle any knots that have developed since I last saw them.

I also try to see newly united moms and daughters around the holidays: Christmas, Thanksgiving, and Mother's Day, all of which can spark problems and hurt feelings. Mother's Day is the worst— every mother is disappointed; every daughter says, "I can't please her"; every Grandma says, "So where are they?" If you know that these flash points are unavoidable, you can plan for them by scheduling a checkup with your therapist in advance of the holiday.

As for the day-to-day tenor of your new relationship, it will be different for each mother and daughter. Some feel most comfortable maintaining a certain amount of distance, and that's fine. I call these *Hallmark relationships,* because the mother and daughter may only touch base on holidays and not communicate much otherwise. But if their former relationship was completely estranged and their connection now is cordial, a Hallmark relationship is a huge improvement.

Like mothers of dissatisfied daughters, you must focus on creating neutral territory in which you and your daughter can relax together. Although you may begin your new relationship with visits to the therapist's office, the goal is to eventually work through your animosity and get to a place where you can enjoy each other's company. The suggestions in chapter nine about finding neutral territory is worthwhile reading for any mom. And the advice I give throughout this book—to accept your daughter for who she is and respect her individuality—must become second nature to you.

As you set out on this journey of reconciliation, be careful, be thoughtful, walk very slowly, and throw away your big stick. There's no room for anger now; what you need is humility. Be thankful if you get the chance to reunite, be tenacious in your efforts to reach your daughter, and be proud of yourself for having the courage to take this trip in the first place. No matter what the outcome, it's worth every ounce of energy you put into it.

PART FIVE

MOVING ON,

TOGETHER OR ALONE

A New Beginning

*I felt like a jilted lover. But in the end, I had to make peace with
the situation; it hurt too much to keep pining for her. To get my
mind off my problems I took an acting class down at the Y. I love
it! It's a real release, and I've even made a few new friends. So it
turns out there is life after Gina. Of course, if she ever calls up, I'll
be thrilled. But my world doesn't depend on it.*

—*M i n n a ,   a g e   s i x t y - t h r e e*

THROUGHOUT THIS BOOK I'VE PREACHED THE GOSPEL OF
individuality. Whether you're repairing your broken bond with a
distant daughter, weaning a dependent daughter from your care,
or establishing new boundaries with a dissatisfied daughter, the
concept of individuality—yours and hers—is key. You can't fix
your daughter's problems or make her happy, and you can't live
your life through her.

No matter what your relationship with your daughter is like,
you are not just a mother, you're a person. You had a life before
you had children, and now that they're grown your life should
continue on its own path. If your dependent or dissatisfied

daughter has become the center of your universe, you must rearrange things so that your needs, not hers, come first. If your daughter is distant, you must realize that she is only one person in your life, one star in your galaxy. You mustn't let her absence snuff out all your light.

This chapter is about nourishing your individuality and charting out your future. In it, I'll share some thoughts about maintaining your new relationship with your daughter; surviving, and even thriving, if she has distanced herself from you; expanding your life beyond the family; and planning for the years ahead.

Mothers' Support Groups

Whether your daughter is dependent, dissatisfied, or distant, joining a mothers' support group is an excellent way to gain solace and inspiration. Long after you've finished reading this book, your daughter will continue to challenge you (to put it kindly). I recommend support groups for all moms with problem children, but especially for those with distant daughters.

The main benefit of these groups is that they keep you from becoming isolated. It's true that you can always talk to your friends—if you're not too ashamed about the situation to confide in them—but friends will eventually grow tired of listening. Their sympathy may warm your heart, but it won't help you solve your problems. Support groups, especially those led by a therapist, will give you an outlet for your feelings and provide the motivation and methods you need to make changes. The groups are not a substitute for friends and family, but an adjunct to them. And there's another advantage to joining a group: when you have a safe place to unload all your "daughter stuff," you'll probably find that your other relationships get a lot more pleasant.

It may be difficult to find a support group in your town that is specifically geared toward mothers of adult daughters, but if so, there's bound to be another type of group that can offer help. As I mentioned in the last chapter, the United Way Info Line has a listing of all the groups in your area. If there are no mothers' groups, you can try two other tacks: women's groups and twelve-step ("Anonymous") groups.

Twelve-step groups offer a straightforward philosophy that has helped millions of people overcome various addictions. But the programs are not just for drug addicts, alcoholics, overeaters, gamblers, and so forth. Groups such as Al-Anon are designed for the families of troubled people; in these groups you'll be able to talk openly about your daughter without feeling embarrassed. The Info Line operator, your clergyperson, or a counselor at the local community center might be able to help you choose an appropriate group from the dozens that meet each week. Twelve-step groups are even listed in the Yellow Pages.

At the heart of the twelve-step philosophy are some concepts similar to the ones I teach my clients. One of these is "Let it go and give it up to God." This doesn't mean that you have no control over your life or that you should relinquish your free will. What it means is that if you dwell on a problem and it handicaps you, you'll never progress past the problem. If you let it go, you can move on. "Giving it up to God" refers to the belief that in order to progress in our lives, we have to accept the fact that some things, like changing a daughter's personality, are beyond our control. They are in the hands of God, or fate, or nature—whatever you want to call it. When we accept our limitations, we're relieved of the impossible task of fixing everyone else. We do have the power to fix ourselves, however, and that's what the twelve steps focus on.

The twelve-step philosophy stresses self-reliance, taking responsibility for your actions, and making amends for your past mistakes. There is also a big emphasis on placing faith in a higher power. The program doesn't favor any specific religion, but the underlying spirituality is what resonates with many members.

Alexandra, sixty-two, found a tremendous amount of support when she joined Al-Anon, a program geared toward the families of people with compulsive behavior. Her daughter was not a compulsive person, but Alexandra still gained a lot from the weekly Al-Anon meetings:

> Every Tuesday night I get to listen to other families' experiences, uncensored. I hear about mothers who have worked through problems with their daughters and sons and husbands, sometimes problems that are much worse than mine. I've been going for about a year and a half now, and these are good, decent people. They understand that I'm not bad, that I'm trying really hard to make things better. And they care about me.
>
> At the end of every meeting we all hold hands and say the Lord's prayer. This has been so incredibly helpful. I'm not a person who can go to church; I stopped a long time ago. Here, though, it feels right.

Members of twelve-step groups have seen and heard it all—whatever you have to say, it's not going to shock them. They warmly welcome anyone in distress, and they won't be pressuring you to reveal anything you don't want to. In fact, many people go to the meetings and say nothing at all for a week or two or three. You don't ever have to speak, if you don't want to—even if you just sit silently at the back of the room, you'll gain insights from hearing about how other people are handling their problems.

If you're uncomfortable with twelve-step groups, you might investigate women's groups instead. These are the descendants of the consciousness-raising groups of the 1970s, and their focus varies widely from group to group. If you join one with women your age, it's quite possible that the subject of families and daughters will be discussed frequently. The drawback is that in many cases there is no philosophical perspective or trained therapist to guide the group, so the conversations tend to wander. Mothers of difficult daughters often need more than just a place to compare notes—they need techniques for dealing with their daughters and improving their lives.

Starting a Mothers' Group

There ought to be a Mothers Anonymous in every city, but right now they are few and far between. If you can't find a mothers' group, you might consider starting one yourself. This doesn't mean you'll have to become a lay psychologist, but you will have to do a little research to find a therapist who can lead the group.

If you and your daughter already see a counselor, begin your search with her. Ask if she'd be interested in leading a mothers' group; if she declines, ask if she knows of another therapist who might be willing to give it a try. If you don't have a therapist, the United Way Info Line can give you the names of those who specialize in family counseling. Call a few and describe what you're looking for. Sooner or later (probably sooner) you'll find one who already has a few clients in the throes of mother-daughter angst. Make it clear to the therapist that you want the group to focus on adult daughters, not teens or young girls. If she seems enthusiastic, set up a meeting with her and ask how she envisions the group. You might also bring a copy of this book and point out the parts that you find particularly useful.

I generally like to keep my mothers' groups small, with a maximum of eight people. Since the sessions last about two hours, this gives everyone enough time to share the week's events and listen to the other members speak. In a small group you get to know the other women fairly quickly, and because of that the discussions can be quite candid. You won't find uncritical support in either twelve-step groups or in smaller mothers' groups; you'll always be expected to look at your own actions honestly and fess up to your mistakes. In exchange, you'll get the compassion and feedback of other women who've walked in your shoes.

Flash Cards

When you first read a self-help book, your mind is ablaze with new ideas that you're raring to put into action. As the weeks and months go by, however, it can be a struggle to remember all the concepts. A few years ago I began to tell mothers to write down key ideas on flash cards—three- by five-inch index cards—so that they'd have ready access to the concepts whenever they needed them. I soon discovered that flash cards were more than a helpful gimmick; they were an invaluable tool for change.

There are several reasons why flash cards work so well when it comes to reinforcing ideas. First, the cards are a handy reference for essential information. Second, there is something mysteriously powerful about the written word. Seeing a written statement packs more punch than merely remembering it; it burns the idea into your mind. Finally, flash cards can coach you in conversations with your daughter. They don't work so well in person: flipping through a stack of flash cards in front of your daughter can come across as either snide or pitiful. Over the phone, however, the cards can be a great help.

Each type of difficult daughter—dissatisfied, dependent, and distant—calls for different flash cards, although some basic statements apply to all. And, of course, every relationship has unique glitches and tender spots. When I see clients in person, I sit down with them and write perhaps twenty-five cards tailored to their situation. You can do this on your own by looking at the list of general statements provided below, choosing those that strike a chord with you, and adding other statements that are especially relevant to you and your daughter.

Flash Cards for All Mothers

- My daughter and I are separate individuals.
- My daughter's problems are hers, not mine.

- I cannot make my daughter happy.
- I will not judge or criticize my daughter.
- I will not ask my daughter prying questions.
- I will not offer unsolicited advice.
- I will not gossip about my daughter to other family members.
- I will not side with any of my children against another child.
- I have no control over my daughter's life.
- I am a person, not just a mother.
- If my daughter can forgive and forget, so can I.
- Cleanliness and Godliness are not the least bit related.
- I do not need to explain myself to my children.
- I will not sacrifice myself for the sake of my children—my name is Mother, not Mother Teresa.
- I will use measured honesty whenever I speak to my daughter. I will tell the truth but do no harm.

Flash Cards for Mothers of Dependent Daughters

- I only need to care about her, not take care of her.
- I will not manipulate anyone because of my daughter's needs or problems.
- My daughter's children are not mine to bring up.
- I will not make excuses for my daughter's behavior.
- Helping my daughter too much will make her more helpless.
- I will decide what gifts to give my daughter based on what I can afford and what I genuinely want to give her.
- I will never give my daughter rent, food, or clothing money but will make any payments directly to the parties owed.
- I will question all reports of mysterious diseases my daughter claims to have.

- I will not cancel my plans because of her latest crisis—there will always be another one.
- I will not deprive myself of necessities in order to give my daughter luxuries.
- I will not put my life on hold while I wait for my daughter to get her act together.
- Dependency is not the same thing as intimacy.

Flash Cards for Mothers of Dissatisfied Daughters

- I cannot change my daughter, but I can change myself.
- Twenty minutes on the phone is enough for God and anyone.
- I will keep my expectations of my daughter within the realm of reality.
- I will not allow my daughter to use me as a dumping ground.
- I will not let my daughter blame me for the turns her life has taken.
- I will not apologize for my accomplishments.
- I can't possibly be wrong all the time—I'll accept 50 percent of the blame.
- Whenever I am tempted to buy my daughter's silence, I will make a donation to a worthy charity instead.

Flash Cards for Mothers of Distant Daughters

- I need to stay away long enough for my daughter to miss me.
- I will allow my daughter the time and space she needs to mature on her own.
- I am a good person, regardless of how my daughter treats me.

- Right and wrong are not important; I only need to agree to disagree.
- I will always try to understand her position.
- I will send cards and notes no matter what she does.
- I will love her always, despite her absence.

When you're talking to your daughter over the phone, think of the flash cards as silent reminders, not scripted dialogue. When you're alone and feeling depressed about her, use the cards to bolster your resolve and remind yourself of your goals. Reading the simple phrase "I can't change my daughter, but I can change myself" can be surprisingly reassuring in times of distress. If nothing else, try the cards for a week or two and see if they help you stay on track. Keep some in your purse, others by the phone. Make several copies of the most important statements and post them around the house—the visual reinforcement helps the message sink in.

The Fountain of Youth: Volunteering

Once you've mapped out a strategy for dealing with your daughter, found a support group, and composed your flash cards, you can turn your attention to the fun stuff—life beyond your problem daughter. There are friends, family, classes, trips, dozens of hobbies and diversions with which to amuse yourself. But before you start scanning the community college catalog or cruise-ship brochures, let me direct you to the most fulfilling activity of all: volunteer work.

"Volunteer? But I don't want to help other people. I want somebody to do something for me." That's the response I sometimes get when I suggest that my clients choose a worthy cause and devote a few hours each week to it.

"You won't only be helping others," I explain. "You'll be helping yourself. Volunteering is the ultimate self-serving activity."

If you think that's just some liberal-do-gooder line, you

couldn't be more wrong. There is no better way to serve yourself a large dose of love, self-esteem, and energy than by volunteering your time to a worthy organization. I should be the nation's poster lady for volunteering, so passionately do I believe in its power to heal the tired and hurting soul. Those of us who devote a lot of time to helping others know the secret: we really do it for ourselves. It feels so good, so life-affirming, that once you get hooked on volunteering you'll never stop.

Volunteering catapults you out of the victim role that many moms wallow in for far too long. Years of self-pity and bitterness can make a person unpleasant to be around. Your friends and family will only want to spend time with you if they enjoy your company; if not, they'll visit you out of a sense of obligation and slip away at the first opportunity. The surest, quickest way to get out from under your dark cloud is to extend your hand to someone needier than yourself. Their gratitude will start to infuse your system immediately, and you'll no longer be so toxic.

When you deliver a batch of homemade soup to the local homeless shelter, plant a garden with a group of schoolchildren, or teach an adult how to read for the first time, you become a different woman than the one who sits at home silently cursing her neglectful daughter. When someone takes your hand and says, "Bless you, thank you, you really came through for us," you feel differently about yourself. The appreciation of those you help will heal you.

You don't have to volunteer in a rape crisis center or a place that frightens or upsets you—opportunities to help are everywhere. Your house of worship, the community or senior center, the United Way, even local newspapers list organizations or events that are seeking volunteer workers. Here is a list to get you thinking, but this is just the tip of the iceberg.

Lend a Helping Hand

- Rock ailing babies at a local hospital.

- Start a garden and grow vegetables to give to a homeless shelter.
- Learn braille and volunteer to transcribe books for the blind, or record tapes for the blind (and get in some fascinating reading for yourself).
- Join a conservation group and help preserve our natural resources.
- Join Habitat for Humanity (the group made famous by former president Jimmy Carter) and help build homes for the needy.
- Join a wildlife preservation group.
- Work on a political campaign.
- Work for a pet adoption agency.
- Become a docent at a museum.
- Volunteer as a teacher's aide, playground assistant, or crossing guard at your local elementary school.
- Become a Little League coach or Scout guide.
- Become a "guardian angel" for an elderly neighbor: offer to drive him or her to the market, doctor's appointments, and so forth.
- Visit the infirm at a nearby residential home, not on the weekends but on lonely Mondays or rainy Tuesdays.
- Collect food for the homeless at your house of worship.
- Become a foster grandparent (United Way has the details).
- Volunteer at your local library.

Bonnie, sixty-three, considered herself an unlikely candidate for volunteer work. "I'm very shy, as bad as a schoolgirl," she confided. "I'm extremely uncomfortable around new people."

"Why not work with children?" I suggested. "They love it any time an adult pays attention to them."

Bonnie agreed somewhat reluctantly to call her local grammar school and ask if they needed help on the playground. To her horror, the principal persuaded her to volunteer as a teacher's aide, reading to second graders every Thursday afternoon.

I was so scared the first time that I literally did not sleep a wink the night before. When I saw the classroom, though, I started to smile—I forgot how little everything is, all the pint-sized chairs and tables. The smallness, and the kids themselves, made me feel more relaxed. The teacher handed me a book, and I started reading. A few pages into it I looked up, and there was this sea of utterly entranced faces hanging on my every word. It hit me that I didn't have to be Meryl Streep to carry this off.

Bonnie now reads in three different classrooms and is known around school as "the story lady." "When I'm not reading, I'm thinking about what I *will* be reading," she told me. "In fact, this got me started on a whole new hobby: collecting vintage children's books. I kept wanting to share the books I had loved as a child, so I started searching used bookstores, flea markets, and yard sales. I've got a pretty good collection now."

Getting involved has a ripple effect, and if you're open-minded it will carry you to places you never knew existed. When you're choosing where to volunteer, think carefully about which causes really appeal to you or can make use of a talent or skill you already possess. That way, your volunteer work is more likely to lead to interesting offshoots.

Broadening Your Horizons

Volunteering is valuable for many reasons, not the least of which is that it's a purely positive action in your life. It will change your perspective on your situation, and it will change people's impressions of you. Should you be concerned what other people think? Yes, if your friends have begun to avoid you because you constantly complain about your daughter. This often happens to mothers of difficult daughters, as I know from personal experience.

In the mid 1970s, when one of my daughters was driving me to near despair, my friend Pattie would patiently listen to my travails. One day, as I launched into yet another tale of my daughter's mishaps, Pattie interrupted me.

"Charney," she said, "Why don't you ever talk about your other kids? You have five, don't you?"

"Well, yes," I admitted. "I guess the squeaky wheel gets the oil."

"That seems so unfair to your other children. Isn't one of your daughters going off to college soon? What about your boys— what are they up to?"

Only then did I see how I had been shortchanging my family by focusing so intently on the difficult daughter. This is typical of what happens when one member of a family has a problem—the problem becomes a black hole, drawing energy away from everyone else. Pattie did me a large favor by pointing this out to me, and she also let me know gently that my laments about my daughter were getting tiresome. Being in therapy or a support group can help you keep your daughter troubles from overshadowing your other relationships: If you can talk about her at length once a week, perhaps you can put her on a back burner the rest of the time.

As you turn your focus away from being just a mom and back toward being a whole person, it's important to reach out to friends and family members with whom you've lost touch. Give them a call and fill them in—briefly—on what you're doing about your daughter problems, then let them know that she will no longer be dominating your conversations. If you haven't spoken to them in a while, your volunteer job will provide a great topic of conversation. By the time they hang up, they'll know they're speaking to a woman who's changing her life for the better. At the end of your chat, if the other person seems glad to hear from you, set up a date with him or her. Slowly, person by person, you need to reconnect with your circle of friends and put an end to your isolation.

Now is also the time to check out classes, hobbies, cultural events, or any other activity you may have considered in the past but had been too depressed to pursue. Pick just one play to attend, or one weekend seminar, and get out into the world. When I see clients in person, I often give them weekly "assignments" to make sure they're being active. These include:

- Call a friend you haven't spoken to in at least one year
- Attend a garden show
- See a play in a small theater or at the local college
- Tour a local landmark
- Take a water-aerobics class
- Join an acting class or theater group
- Learn to use a computer and "surf the web" (I started at age sixty-eight)
- Start a quilting bee
- Usher at the philharmonic
- Take tap-dance lessons
- Hike with Sierra Club Seniors
- Join the Sweet Adelines or sing in the chorus of a local musical production
- Start a book club
- Become an artist, using pencil, brush, pastels—or welding torch

There is one assignment I give every mom who has a backyard: Plant a garden. Nurturing a garden is tremendously satisfying for all mothers who miss tending a family, but it's particularly therapeutic for mothers of distant daughters. Plants may not give you a Mother's Day card, but if you care for them, they respond beautifully. You'll also learn to sow seeds and leave them alone long enough to germinate and thrive—a good metaphor for raising a family and waiting out a distant daughter's return.

Adopting a Family

A number of years ago I became aware of a small trend among my clients. Because Los Angeles is a magnet for people from all over the country and the world, many who live here don't have relatives in town. Some of the moms I was counseling began to mention getting together for holidays with a young family down the block, or a single mom from the office, or the twenty-something couple next door. Time and again these clients would joke, "They're my adopted family." Dee Dee, seventy-four, was one of these clients.

Dee Dee had endured a serious falling-out with her daughter Marla after Dee Dee's husband, Richard, confessed to a fifteen-year affair with another woman. Dee Dee sent Richard packing, but instead of supporting her decision, Marla withdrew. "She thinks I should have somehow worked things out with Richard," Dee Dee told me, "but the real problem is that she's scared—she doesn't want to have to take care of me when I get old. So she told me that unless I'd reconcile with her father, she wouldn't have anything to do with me. Marla always was intimidated by her dad," Dee Dee mused. "He turned her against me, but she was willing to be turned. I've accepted the fact that she's gone, probably for good, and I'm not expecting any miracles."

Six years after Richard and Marla exited, Dee Dee was living a better life than she ever had before. She'd always been outgoing, but now she blossomed. She held a job as an assistant chef in one of her town's most prestigious restaurants, and her social calendar was always full. It never would have occurred to her to "adopt" a child, but then:

I was at a play and happened to sit next to a very charming young man of about twenty-five. It turned out that he was from Lebanon and was here to study at the Culinary

Institute of California, then go into the restaurant business. Massal and I clicked right away. He told me he missed his family a lot, so I invited him to dinner. The moment he walked into my house I said, "You know, if this evening goes well I'm adopting you."

We've been pals ever since. A middle-aged lady from the suburbs and a twenty-five-year-old man—my friends may think I'm crazy, but he and I get along like fireworks. Every few weeks we have dinner together, and sometimes we go dancing at a Middle Eastern restaurant. He's the son any mother would love to have. Massal is very devoted to his own parents, which makes me like and respect him all the more. We fill a space in each other's lives—this is a treat I never thought I'd experience.

Vanessa, sixty-seven, adopted an entire family. "They're a young couple from Georgia who live three doors down from me," Vanessa explained. "I saw them strolling their new baby by my house and stopped to comment on how beautiful he was. The next week they invited me over for dinner, and it just grew from there. I baby-sit for them sometimes, and they include me in all their activities. The baby even calls me Grandma."

Dee Dee and Vanessa's "adoptions" occurred accidentally, but there is no reason why you can't consciously seek out someone to connect with. It could be a couple at your house of worship or community center, a teacher at your grandchild's preschool, or someone you meet through your volunteer job. I myself have an adopted son (even though my own two sons are very attentive, I had room for one more). He was on the catering staff at my sixty-fifth birthday party. After the party he asked if he could take a swim in my pool, and I said, "Sure—anytime." Michael was such an outgoing, affable person that I was happy to invite him into my home. Since then he's gotten married and had a child; now the whole family is a part of my life.

I'm not suggesting that adopted families can take the place of blood relations. But believe it or not, in some respects they're more rewarding than real families. Over the years you build up a history with your adopted family with a sense of dedication and devotion.

Adopted families are especially enjoyable during the holidays. You get to share all the togetherness and festivity that the occasion calls for without the angst that plagues so many real families in the holiday season. And with relatives so far-flung, it's wonderful to host or attend a celebration that's down the block rather than four states away.

Be Prepared!

Without question, it's going to be daunting to try to put into action all the suggestions in this book. Once you make the commitment to do it, however, you'll quickly begin to see changes in your life. In about four to six months, when you've gotten used to your new routine, you'll be ready to put the final pieces in place: preparing for the future. You—not your children—are the only one who should make these preparations. The quality of your life is at stake, and right now, while you're still energetic, is the time to get your house in order.

Mothers of my generation tend to assume that if we were good role models and took care of our aging parents, our children will follow suit. But there is no guarantee that our kids will come to our rescue. No one wants to be dependent on her children but, in fact, it might not even be an option. If our kids live in another city, or in a home that's not large enough to accommodate an extra person, or if they can't afford another mouth to feed, we have big decisions ahead of us.

"I had to move my ninety-four-year-old mother into a nursing facility this summer," Lonnie, seventy-one, told my mothers' group one day. As Lonnie described her sense of obligation and worries about the future, the rest of us nodded in sympathy. We knew that we, too, would be facing these problems some day.

> I hated to put Mother in a home, but after she fractured her hip I had no choice. I spent the entire summer cleaning up her apartment, wading through thirty years' worth of old greeting cards, letters, check stubs, and receipts. She never even thanked me. I'm an only child, so the entire burden of her care fell on me. Yet even though my mother is hard to manage, I'm proud of the fact that I've done right by her. I've fulfilled my daughterly obligation, and I'm not sorry. She deserves my help—after all, she is my mother.

Although this scenario is not perfect, Lonnie could live with it except for one thing: She's afraid her own daughter will not do the same for her. "Who will take care of me when I'm old?" she wonders—along with nearly every other woman I counsel. We all feel vulnerable and frightened about the prospect of growing old alone. In fact, many of the women I know tell me they have a secret fear of ending up a homeless bag lady.

The only way to conquer this fear is to take control of your own future. Make certain, to the best of your ability, that you will not be dependent upon your children. Even if you have five wonderful kids, as I do, it is up to you to take responsibility for your later years. For starters, find out where the nearest senior center is. Unless you're wealthy, get information about HUD housing for the elderly (and get on a HUD waiting list *now;* it can take years for a spot to open up). Make inquiries into the application process for assisted-living facilities. There are many appealing alternatives for seniors, and volumes of information are available at the library.

Don't be caught off guard by the natural process of aging; keep one step ahead of it. Clean out drawers and closets and start to distribute mementos and heirlooms now, so you can enjoy the delights of giving and see your children's faces as they receive your treasures.

Figure out how long your money will last and how far your retirement benefits will take you. Take classes, read books, investi-

A Little Peek in the Crystal Ball

Having a hard time relating to an older version of you? Maybe this exercise will help. Imagine yourself at eighty, and ask yourself the following questions:

- How do you look?
- How do you feel physically?
- What city and state are you living in?
- What is your financial situation?
- What are your interests?
- What is your state of mind? Are you happy or sad? Fearful or trusting? Content or resentful?
- What are your favorite pastimes?
- Do you have any companions?
- Are you actively pursuing your interests, or are you waiting for someone to come get you?
- Do you see your children?
- Do you have a pet?
- What have you done for someone else lately?

If you can't visualize the answers to some of these questions, or if your answers scare you, you need to start your plan for the future. Get help if you need it, but take those first steps now. The library is a wonderful place to begin.

gate all the government programs. Take charge, and when you have a clear picture, take a vacation. Spend some of that money you were going to leave to your kids, and use the rest to set up your future. Take control while you can.

In my experience, children are delighted when their parents travel or splurge, even if it means some of the inheritance money will be spent. They're thrilled to see Mom and Dad enjoying themselves—it sends a positive message about growing older. I am the therapist the kids go to when Mom dies, and they are often anguished about inheriting her savings. "Why didn't she have more fun if she had all this money?" they ask me. I can only answer, "She did it for you. She didn't know any better—she was a Depression baby."

Times have changed. What you see as duty toward your children, they may view as excessive self-sacrifice. And the obligatory care you expect from them may be beyond their capacity to give. So face your future head-on, and once you have a clear sense of your options, enjoy the present!

Wiping the Slate Clean

We've all been hurt. Getting past the hurts that damn us, that saddle us with angst, regrets, and ill will—that's the stage we aspire to. In this book I've distilled the knowledge I've gained from twenty-five years of clinical practice, in the hopes that mothers and daughters can shed their hurts and anger for the sake of a new beginning with each other. Like the hundreds of women I have counseled, you too can change your behavior, expectations, and relationship with your daughter—you can change your life. *Only* you can do it.

At the end of chapter one, I gave you the Mother's Bill of Rights, a list of the inalienable rights all mothers should claim as their own. I'd like to close this final chapter with another list—or rather, two of them. These are the ten commandments for mothers and daughters. Follow them, pray a little, forgive a lot, and good luck!

Mother's Ten Commandments

1. Thou shalt not covet thy daughter's body, money, or maid.

2. Thou shalt not judge or criticize thy daughter's behavior.

3. Thou shalt not override thy daughter's rules in her own home.

4. Thou shalt not question thy daughter's lifestyle or personal choices.

5. Thou shalt love thy daughter even if she is nothing at all like you.

6. Thou shalt not make promises to your daughter that you cannot fulfill.

7. Thou shalt not carry tales about your daughter to anyone.

8. Thou shalt always use measured honesty when speaking with your daughter.

9. Thou shalt not speak against thy daughter's mate or his family.

10. Thou shalt respect thy daughter as you would wish her to respect you.

Daughter's Ten Commandments

1. Thou shalt not covet thy mother's possessions, money, or freedom.

2. Thou shalt not expect thy mother to support you financially.

3. Thou shalt not make demands upon thy mother, only polite requests.

4. Thou shalt not neglect or abuse thy mother.

5. Thou shalt never assume you know thy mother's thoughts or feelings.

6. Thou shalt not deny your mother the right to visit with your children.

7. Thou shalt remember thy mother on holidays.

8. Thou shalt not criticize thy mother's lifestyle, attire, spending, or eating habits.

9. Thou shalt assist thy mother in times of personal crisis.

10. Thou shalt respect thy mother as you would wish her to respect you.

And Now, a Word from Our Daughters

THROUGHOUT THIS BOOK I'VE TRIED TO BE EVENHANDED in my advice to mothers. I've presented both the mothers' and daughters' sides of the story, but because I am a mothers' advocate, I've naturally focused on the mom's point of view. Still, I hope that one underlying truth has come through: Mothers and daughters are equals in their need for each other. As much as you have worried and mourned for your daughter, she has probably anguished and longed for you.

Here, then, as a final note of encouragement, are some stories of renewal and reconciliation from the daughters' point of view.

"Mom Loved My Sister Best"

ELLEN, AGE FIFTY-FOUR

My mother always loved my sister best, or so I thought. Mom cooed over Alice, talked incessantly about her success in school and, later on, her astounding career accomplishments. I felt like the meek brown wren next to my sister, the swan.

Even though she eventually moved fifteen hundred miles away, it was as if my sister were present at every family event. Mom would spend the whole time updating the family on Alice's degrees, awards, and so on. She bragged about her constantly.

Alice left home when she was eighteen and I was twelve, and all my youth I resented her.

I never left my hometown, and when I was twenty-six I had my first child. Mom was at my side day and night. She was my main support system, there for me no matter what. It was then, twenty-eight years ago, that I realized how much my mother had loved me all along. In fact, I began to feel like the favored one! My sister didn't need Mom, and Mom liked to be needed. It made her feel important. After all those years of thinking I was "less than," I reveled in my mother's love and attention. So, regardless of how we got there, my mother and I became very close.

I'm friends with my sister, too, but she and I are extremely different. She's an entrepreneur, ultrasuccessful, and I'm a homemaker with a part-time job. When Mom became ill with diabetes she turned to me, and I was happy to help her. I'm sorry now that I resented her affection for my sister, but I'm glad that we got it all straightened out and were able to enjoy so many years together. I was with my mother when she died; my sister was on a lecture tour.

"I Never Fit In"

MARIE-LOUISE, AGE THIRTY-SIX

"Who's my real mother?" I used to ask my Nana. "Am I adopted? Did my real mom die?" If my mother had ever heard those questions it would've broken her heart! Luckily Nana never told.

I honestly thought I must be adopted—that's how much I didn't fit into my family. I didn't know then that lots of immigrants' kids feel this way. I only knew that my mother was different than me, and different than the other mothers I knew. She spoke with a strong guttural accent, which was embarrassing enough, but in addition to that she was sort of a walking disaster area. (Sorry, Mom.) The house was a mess, she fried everything she cooked, and she spent all her time racing around but never getting anything done. That's the way it seemed to me, anyhow, through my teenage eyes. I couldn't stand to be around her, much less introduce her to any of my friends.

It all changed when we moved to another city. Being sixteen, I was almost out of the house by then, and I left for college as soon as I could. But while I was gone, Mom started to observe American ways. She started to assimilate, something I thought she'd never do. She took classes at the local high school at night, and even changed her cooking habits. She started to play bridge and do volunteer work. Slowly her accent faded, and in a subtle way she began to transition into the mother I had always wanted.

Mom will never be the sophisticated matron who dines at the Ritz, but neither will I. I realize now that I was judgmental and hypercritical of her long after I was grown up enough to know better. The most important thing is the way a mother parents you, not the clothes she's wearing when she does it. I was loved, cared for, and despite my disdain for my mother, she accepted me unconditionally. I only hope I can treat my children as well as she treated me.

"Dad Died and I Hated Mom"

FRANCES, AGE THIRTY-EIGHT

My dad died when I was thirteen. He had a heart attack and died in the hospital that same day. I saw the priest come to the house with my mother and knew immediately that my father was dead; I started to sob and didn't stop for hours. My father was my favorite person in the whole world, the center of my life. I looked and acted just like him, which people used to comment about all the time.

When he died a part of me died too, and I blamed my mother.

If she had taken better care of him he wouldn't have died, I used to tell myself. She should have made him stop eating junk food, she should have made him stop yelling, she should have made him take things easier. He worked too hard, his hours were too long; in fact, we hardly ever saw him.

For years I blamed my mother for his passing and made her life a living hell. I aimed all my fury at her—I didn't consider for a minute how she must be feeling. I really wanted her to die. It took me many years of loneliness and despair to realize that it was actually my father I was angry at for not taking care of himself. I started to see this truth after joining Overeaters Anonymous, a twelve-step program. In those meetings I learned that children often blame the functional parent for the mistakes of the dysfunctional one. Of course Dad wasn't really dysfunctional—just a workaholic, type-A personality. Still, it took me ten years to realize that I had been blaming my mother for the way my father lived his life.

When Dad died Mom was left alone to bring up four kids. I never thought about her at all, only myself and my pain. I'm so thankful that I finally woke up and started to mend my relationship so that we've now had nine great years together, and hopefully we'll have many more. Mom never stopped loving me through all those troubled years, and I marvel at that. A mother's love is truly a special thing. I try to make it up to her in any way that I can for those bad times I gave her. I know she has forgiven me, but I have a hard time forgiving myself.

"I Punished My Parents for Getting Divorced"

BRITTE, AGE TWENTY-NINE

My parents got a divorce when I was twenty-two, and I was devastated. I could not understand how they could do this to me. After thirty-five years of marriage, they broke up our family without even discussing it with us kids. When I asked them why they were splitting up, they just said that it was personal and they didn't want to talk about it.

At the time I couldn't get it out of my head that they were doing this *to* me. I decided to get even with them by rejecting them both. I moved across country and didn't speak to my mother or father for about five years.

Little did I realize that my parents had only stayed together all those years for the sake of us children, and now that we were all out of the house they felt free to make new lives for themselves. I might have stayed away forever, except that my sister got married. At the wedding I saw that my parents both had new partners and seemed quite happy. My brothers and sisters had been seeing Mom and Dad all the while I had been gone from the family. I had missed out on all the holidays and celebrations; meanwhile, Mom and Dad had remained friends! All the time I thought I was punishing them, I had been depriving myself of my family. I was the one with the problem.

I felt pretty ashamed for being so obtuse about their breakup, but thank God I came to my senses in time. Now we celebrate the holidays as a large, blended family, something that's unusual these days, when so many divorced couples dislike each other. I'll never quite understand how my parents stayed together all those years if they didn't love each other, but I'm able to accept it as a sacrifice they made for us kids. I'm grateful for the happy childhood they gave me.

"I Wanted Dad for Myself"

KAY, AGE FORTY-FOUR

Daddy's girl—what's so bad about that? I loved being a daddy's girl. There was only one thing wrong with the picture, and that was Mom. Even though I was the apple of my daddy's eye, ultimately *she* had him, and I resented her for it. He slept with her, ate with her, went out with her, and—I had to admit—loved her and was dedicated to her. Why her, why not me? I was younger, cuter, smarter, always available. All of my love and longing for Dad was right on the surface; I did nothing to hide my contempt for my mother.

As far as I was concerned, Mom was the enemy. I created some pretty ugly scenes, calling her names and ridiculing her, often in front of Dad. He never stopped me—I think they were both at a loss about how to handle me. Who knows what was going on between the two of them, what part I played in any power trips happening there. As far as I could tell, they had decided to just wait it out until I left home.

I left at seventeen, totally confused and frustrated by my futile attempts to woo Dad away from Mom. I went off to college, never to return. In the following years I got involved in many destructive love affairs with awful men who treated me badly, exploited me—there was even one loser who stole my car! After that incident I started seeing a therapist to figure out why I kept getting involved with these creepy guys. Eventually I realized that I was punishing myself for not being "good enough" to get Dad away from Mom.

I think that I had to grow up and put a certain distance between me and my family before I could come to terms with any of this. When the fog finally cleared, I realized that I had had this loving mother all those years and I didn't even acknowledge her presence, only prayed for her absence.

I'm still shocked that I ever managed to marry a healthy, relatively normal man. But I did, and we've got two sons. Here's a secret I've never told anyone: I'm really relieved I don't have any daughters! I'd never want to go through what I put my mother through.

I see a lot of my parents now. Mom and I have never discussed the past, but we love spending time together. She taught me how to be a good mother, and she's a wonderful grandmother, too.

"Mom Has Changed"

DANIELLE, AGE TWENTY

My mother was the perfect mom. I used to love it when I came home and smelled the cookies she had baked, and sometimes she'd even have art projects all set up and ready for me and my friends to work on. She studied different types of cuisine—Asian, French, Mediterranean—so we always had a gourmet chef at our beck and call. My room was neat, my clothes were laundered and ironed. My life was ideal.

Then, when I was in junior high school, my mom went to college and began to work toward a degree. I hated her for that. She stopped cooking all those gourmet meals, stopped driving me everywhere I asked, and told me I had to do my own laundry. I felt like I had lost my mother—now she spent all her time studying.

I stayed sullen and angry at her for years. Then, when I went to college myself, I began to see her in a different light. When I met all these girls from other states and we talked about our moms, I realized that most of them had worked. My mom was the rarity. I had had what amounts to a personal maid. I was almost embarrassed to admit how much my mother had done for my brother and me, and I sure didn't let on how mad I had been when she decided to go to college.

On my first trip back home, I let my mother know how sorry I was for treating her so badly. Now that I was in college too, I realized how hard it must have been for her to go to school and still keep the house together. I helped her study during my visits, and even typed a few of her term papers. That was quite a switch, me helping Mom!

I learned a lot from those girls in my dorm. They were further along than I was; now I feel as if I've caught up. Mom and I are in college at the same time, and I'm really proud of her. We're closer than ever, and it keeps getting better.

"Mom Disapproved of My Religion"

REBECCA, AGE THIRTY-NINE

I stopped speaking to my mother about eight years ago, when I converted to Orthodox Judaism. I'd been raised in a Reform household, where we went to temple for the big holidays but that was all. We never prayed at home; in fact, Judaism was treated more as a matter of race and culture than as a religion.

When I converted I knew my mother would be surprised. Dad had died several years earlier, and I thought maybe she'd like to explore my new belief system, but instead she rejected it and me. I invited her to join me at services and to visit my new neighborhood (located walking distance from the synagogue), but she actually scoffed at me. "You and I are so different now, I just can't adjust," she said. I couldn't understand her antipathy, and I imagine she couldn't understand my rejection of her values.

I hoped things would improve over time, but for a long while they only got worse. Mom treated my conversion as if it were some trivial fad. She criticized my kosher food observances, feeling insulted that I wouldn't eat at her house. She called me dowdy because the clothing I now wore covered my arms and legs and was not revealing. Suddenly there was this tremendous gulf between us, and it seemed to me that Mother did very little to try to bridge it. For instance, she'd always ask me over to her house on Saturday, knowing full well that according to Orthodox law it's a sin to drive or carry money on the Sabbath. Mom never got it; rather, she railed against my observances and distanced herself from me. Gradually we stopped talking to each other, except for a few brief phone calls a year.

We were at a stalemate until I decided to marry my longtime beau and called to tell her the news. She was ambivalent. "Does this mean I'll see even less of you?" she demanded.

Maybe because getting married was such an important event for me, I had vowed to try once again to win my mother over.

"Please, Mom," I said. "Come stay with me this Saturday. You can spend Friday night at my house, and we'll go to services together. Then you can see what my life is all about now, and meet David, too."

She finally accepted. I believe this was because so much time had passed—five years—that she realized I was committed to my new faith. That made her a little more willing to listen when I explained about the laws of purity and the observance of the Sabbath, with all the beauty that involved. The ability to put aside everyday concerns and spend twenty-four hours in prayer truly impressed my mother. She saw the peace and tranquillity in me and my fiancé, and how all our friends gathered at the Oneg Shabbat to study and pray together.

Rather than scoff at my new life, my mother began to participate in some of it, although she never expressed the desire to convert and we never pushed her. She was thrilled to take part in our wedding ceremony, and of course she was ecstatic when she realized that David and I wanted a big family. We have three children now, and Mother is often at our house. We are always careful to respect one another's differences and not take our relationship for granted. There were a few years when I felt I had lost Mom for good, and I thank the Lord that we're reunited again.

"My Glamorous Mother Had No Time for Me"

ROCHELLE, AGE TWENTY-FOUR

My mother was a concert pianist, glamorous, beautiful, and sophisticated. She was never home, and when she was, she was too busy for me. Instead of having a normal childhood, I was raised by nannies and maids.

Mother traveled the world giving concerts, and I was not permitted to go along. My father was my mother's agent, and he traveled with her, so for most of my childhood neither parent was around. Sometimes, in between tours, the three of us would take a vacation together. They always took my nanny too, because they were so busy throwing parties or attending dinners in their honor that even on vacation I was excluded.

I always thought my mother deliberately chose to leave me and travel so much, until one day she explained her life to me. I was fifteen years old and miserably unhappy. On one of her weeklong stopovers at our house, I gathered all my courage and approached her. "I want to leave home and go to a boarding school," I announced. "I don't guess it'll matter much to you and Dad, but I'm really unhappy and I don't want to live with you anymore."

Mom turned pale and just stared at me sadly for a long time. Then she said, "Rochelle, I'm so sorry. I honestly had no idea you were unhappy. Believe me, there are reasons for the way we live. I guess you're old enough now to know what they are."

My mother told me that she and Dad had made a pact years ago, when they found out he had a degenerative illness that would probably alter his life at a relatively young age. She'd be the breadwinner—as a world-class pianist, she could command much more money that he would have been able to earn at a regular job—and he would be her agent. She'd work as hard as she could and accumulate as much money as possible for them to live on when Dad's illness got bad. Mom told me that she hated to leave me so much but was terrified that she wouldn't be able to save enough before she was forced to stop touring. "New young talents are coming up all the time. Who knows how long people will pay to hear me?" she asked. "Or how long I'll have the energy to keep doing this?"

It had never occurred to me that my glamour mom could wear down or get tired. She seemed invincible. And she told me that I had always acted so self-contained and independent that she never thought I really needed her. Here we were, both covering up our weaknesses and not revealing our true feelings. We learned a lot about each other that day—I only wish I had tried to leave home sooner!

Now that I'm older I play the piano with Mom. We do duets and I love listening to her CDs. I appreciate her talent now, rather than resent it, and I understand why she did what she did. I understand the part she didn't say, too: when you've got all that talent, it would be incredibly hard not to give concerts and revel in the praise and appreciation of people all over the world. I still wish she had spent more time with me, but I believe her when she says she felt like she had no choice.

Mom plans to retire from traveling next year and start to teach at a local university. Fortunately Dad is still with us although, as the doctors predicted, he's very limited in what he can do. Our family is small, but at least we've got each other.

"My Mother Abandoned Me"

CHARNEY, AGE SIXTY-EIGHT

My beloved mother, to whom I've dedicated this book, was a remarkable woman. But she and I had a shaky beginning, which took me many years to understand. She passed away in 1995 at the age of eighty-three, and I'm forever indebted to her for teaching me the value of a generous spirit and forgiving heart.

I never really felt comfortable with my mother, and I didn't know why. Dad was always hugging and kissing us kids, but Mom always seemed to be preoccupied. I felt uneasy and mistrustful about her, and I could never figure out why I had those feelings. The only clue I had was a vague memory that didn't make much sense. It was a memory of something that had happened when I was very small, and it was so sketchy that I thought it might be a fantasy and not a real memory at all. This trace memory reemerged quite often, always filling me with feelings of sadness and dread. I didn't dare ask my mother about it, but I longed to find out if it was fact or fiction.

Finally, when I was forty years old, I visited my hometown and saw my aging aunt and uncle at a family gathering. I resolved to ask Aunt Dottie about the memory that haunted me. I recalled it to her in vivid detail: I was about two years old and was being taken by someone (Aunt Dottie and Uncle Harry, as it turned out) to see my mother. She worked in a resort in the Watchung mountains as a baby-sitter. We drove there in a big old green car, a Nash, with hard leather seats and a little round window in the back.

My mother had left my brother and me with Aunt Dottie that summer and gone to work at the resort. When we drove up, she rushed to greet us, then took me into the lake to swim and hug and kiss me. How I loved being held by her! I missed her so much and I was so little. Later that day my aunt and uncle took me away from my mother—they had to tear me out of her arms. I can still hear myself screaming for her. Aunt Dottie kept saying that we had to leave because it was such a long ride home. All the way back to the city, I sat alone in that big back seat sobbing.

Even as I write this today, I can't help but cry at the pain that separation caused me. I think I must have wept for days, but then, as rejected babies do, I gave up. I entered a state of anaclitic depression, the depression of abandonment. For much of my life I suffered from separation anxiety and feared strange or new situations. I also had a hard time trusting women, and never felt close to my mother.

When I told Aunt Dottie about my memory of the lake, she was dumbfounded. She confirmed the whole thing, but said, "Who told you about that? You were never supposed to know. Your mother was gone for six months, and when she came back she made us all swear never to tell you that she had left you when you were so young." No one had told me, I assured her. I had remembered it.

A little while after this discussion with Aunt Dottie, I decided to confront my mother about why she had left. I planned a shopping foray with her, to be followed by lunch. My idea was to ask her everything over that meal, but to my astonishment, she spontaneously opened the subject herself. "There are some things I need to tell you," she began. It was incredible. I had to ask her nothing: we were on the same wavelength.

My mother told me that when I was two and my brother was four, my father had left her and gone to Spain (he came back to the family two years later). She was lonely—a poor, uneducated teenager saddled with two small children and no hope for the future. Her older sister worked at the Watchung resort as an entertainer and was leading a glamorous life, and my mother wanted to have some fun too. She had felt cheated out of her childhood, and left us to recover part of her lost youth. She soon returned home, guilt ridden and worried because I had fallen into an almost autistic state.

After she revealed her long-kept secret, my mother asked for my forgiveness. We both cried, and of course I forgave her. I finally understood what had happened, what had caused the abandonment. Mom and I were close from that day forward, and I eventually learned to trust women and get over my separation anxiety. I will admit, though, that I still cry whenever I relive that memory, because although I have forgiven, I have not forgotten. I wish I could, for I loved my mother very much and miss her every day. I'm so grateful we worked out our problems in time to enjoy many wonderful years together.

Resources

....

NOTE: Some organizations have only local listings. Please consult your phone directory for resource listings in your area.

Alanon	818-760-7122
Alateen	818-508-8301
Because I Love You	310-659-5289
Cocaine Anonymous	800-347-8998
Dept. of Human Resources	818-596-4444
Dept. of Rehabilitation	818-901-5024
Elder Hostel	617-426-8056
Families Anonymous	800-736-9805
Family Friends	818-761-3447
	(Adoptive Grandparents)
Habitat for Humanity	800-422-4828
Housing and Urban	
Development	818-342-7176
Job Corps	800-562-2677
Overeater's Anonymous	818-881-4776 and
	818-342-2222
Narcotics Anonymous	818-787-7189
Recording for the Blind	800-732-8398
Sierra Club	415-977-5500
Sweet Adelines	818-761-7464
Tough Love	800-339-6993
Tree People	310-753-4600
United Way-Info Line	800-339-6993

References

Adler, Tina. "Comprehending Those Who Can't Relate." *Science News,* April 16, 1994, pp. 248–49.

Azar, Beth. "Nature, nurture: not mutually exclusive." *The APA [American Psychological Association] Monitor,* May 1997.

Bouchard, Thomas J. "Genes, Environment, and Personality." *Science,* June 17, 1994, pp. 1700–1.

Cordes, Helen. "There's No Such Thing as a Mothering Instinct." *Utne Reader,* September/October 1994, pp. 15–16.

Corelli, Ray. "Get Happy." *Maclean's,* September 16, 1996, pp. 54–57.

"The Despised Office of Motherhood." *Journal of the American Medical Association,* April 17, 1996.

Gallagher, Winifred. "How We Become What We Are." *The Atlantic Monthly,* September 1994, pp. 39–55.

Martensen, Robert L. "Physiology as Destiny: Medicine and Motherhood in the Progressive Era." *Journal of the American Medical Association,* April 17, 1996.

"Thanks, Mum." *The Economist,* November 4, 1995, pp. 87–88.

Wright, Lawrence. "Double Mystery." *The New Yorker,* August 7, 1995, pp. 45–62.

ABOUT THE AUTHORS

DR. CHARNEY HERST is director of Psychotherapy Associates, a clinical practice in Encino, California. A licensed marriage and family therapist with a Ph.D. in clinical psychology, she specializes in relationships with an emphasis on the bond between mother and daughter. Dr. Herst is a seminar leader in the Wagner Program at the University of Judaism in Los Angeles, past president of the board of directors of the San Fernando Valley Counseling Center, and the community affairs chairperson of Valley Outreach Synagogue, where she was recipient of the Woman of the Year award for 1998. She has three daughters, two sons, and eight grandchildren, and lives with her husband and childhood sweetheart, Simon Buchsbaum, and their collie, Lacey, in Los Angeles.

LYNETTE PADWA is the author of *Everything You Pretend to Know and Are Afraid Someone Will Ask* (Penguin, 1996). She is a fifteen-year veteran of the West Coast book publishing industry and has worked as a freelance writer-editor since 1991. She lives in Los Angeles with her husband and son.

ABOUT THE TYPE

This book was set in Bembo, a typeface
based on an old-style Roman face that
was used for Cardinal Bembo's tract
De Aetna in 1495. Bembo was cut by
Francisco Griffo in the early sixteenth
century. The Lanston Monotype Machine
Company of Philadelphia brought the
well-proportioned letter forms of Bembo
to the United States in the 1930s.